Scaredy Dog!

In Memory of
"Montana"
Border Collie Mix
HIC, CGC, TDIAOV, R1CL, R2MCL

Scaredy Dog!

Understanding and Rehabilitating Your Reactive Dog.

Ali Brown, M.Ed., CPDT, CDBC

Published by Tanacacia Press
Great Companions
P.O. Box 36
Neffs, PA 18065
www.greatcompanions.info

ISBN 13: 978-0-9766414-0-7

Cover Design: Pete Smoyer, e-Production
All Photography: Pete Smoyer
Manufactured in the United States of America

Dedicated to Acacia

CONTENTS

PREFACE

This updated version of *Scaredy Dog!* is not a complete rewrite of the original, but rather a clarified version of it. Time goes by, thoughts become clearer, ideas change, and so after five years, I decided that the book needed spiffing up. While it is still designed to be a quick read, I cleaned up some of the writing, included more specific examples, and added more and better photos to give you a better idea of what to look for and how to handle your dog.

I hope that you find this book to be of help to you and your beloved companion. So many of us are at a complete loss as to how to go about affecting change within our dogs, and it can be very frustrating when all we wanted was a pet, not a project.

Enjoy the read. When I first wrote the book, there was little available as a resource to owners of reactive dogs; now there are quite a few books and DVDs out there. If you devour this volume and are desperate for more, my second book *Focus Not Fear* would be the next in a logical step of self-help books for you and your reactive dog. *Focus Not Fear* documents the range of class and individual exercises I use to help people moderate their dog's reactivity. In addition, there is a companion DVD to *Scaredy Dog!* from a seminar I held in Phoenix, Arizona. Both *Focus Not Fear* and the *Scaredy Dog! Seminar DVD* are available through Dogwise.com.

Thanks
Ali

INTRODUCTION

OK. So your dog lunges at people and other dogs when he's on the leash. He goes ballistic when people come to the door, snarling and throwing saliva everywhere. The smallest sound is enough to get him going for hours…well, OK, ten minutes. But it still drives you crazy! Or he alternatively hides from and barks at visitors to your home. You can't take him anywhere because he makes such a scene. People walk the other way when they see you and Buddy coming. They don't want to be anywhere near that frothy animal! And heaven forbid someone should turn the corner quickly on your walk and suddenly appear…he might get nipped or bitten (or your arm might get ripped out of the socket!) This is not what dog ownership is supposed to be! HELP!!!!!

I can do that for you! Actually, with you…

CANIS FAMILIARIS

First, we need to know a little more about dogs and why they do things. You can pick up any book on dog training these days and read about how dogs are social animals, den animals, live in a social hierarchy, do best when they have a leader, don't generalize well, and have superior sensory abilities compared to humans. So I won't go into much detail about any of these here. If any of those descriptions surprise you, you might do well to buy and read a more basic book before reading this one.*

Dogs thrive when they have a safe place to call theirs (our modern-day version of "den" is "crate"). This is where they will go when they are tired, not feeling well, or need to "get away from it all." It should also be the place your dog spends his time when you are not there to supervise him. A nervous dog often will do better in a crate when alone than wandering around the house, looking for comfort. Indeed, many dogs seem to have forgotten, or never knew, that a consistent, cozy resting place can be a calming respite. Having said that, some dogs have a tendency toward separation anxiety or true separation anxiety. In the former case, it is imperative to teach the dog that great things happen in the crate, and that he will be fine when he is alone. In the latter case, a much more intense training program is needed, and the dog may benefit from medication prescribed by your veterinarian. This is the only situation in which a crate is often counterproductive. We will discuss crating in more detail later.

Because dogs are pack animals, they are, by definition, social animals. This means that they enjoy being with similar others. If other

---

* THE DOG'S MIND, by Bruce Fogle, DVM, 1990, Howell Book House, is a nice introduction to the world of the dog.

dogs aren't available, humans, or sometimes even cats, will do. Since we have domesticated dogs (or more likely, they've domesticated themselves), we humans will suffice for pack animals. This means that we are part of their social hierarchy. But that does not mean that we need to be "dominant" over our dogs, nor do our dogs need to be "submissive" or "subservient" toward us. Simply put, we need to help the dog to understand that the humans in the family have the big brain and the opposable thumbs, and all humans in the house are "benevolent leader." We humans are able to provide all of the things in our dogs' lives that they perceive as wonderful: food, car rides, access to outside, chew toys, the throwing of tennis balls, the use of tug toys, scratching and petting, and the list, of course, goes on. It is mostly on this principle that success in our relationship with our dogs relies. More on that later.

Dogs are, much to our dismay, far superior to humans in many ways. They hear better than we do. They run faster than we do. Indeed, even the smallest dog will pull on its leash, proving that those with four legs can move faster than those with two! It has been estimated that a male dog can smell a female dog in season (estrus) over a mile away; this information has been extrapolated and translated into the estimate that a dog's sense of smell is one million times better than ours. Dogs have 220 million scent receptors, while humans have a paltry five million. Dogs can see better than we can in three out of five ways. First, they have better peripheral vision. We have about 180 degrees; they have about 270 degrees, depending on the breed. Second, they have better motion perception, and third, they have better night vision (dogs have a double retina, or tapetum, which permits light two opportunities to get through; this is why dogs' eyes "glow" at night). However, we are better able to detect objects at a distance. If you were to stand perfectly still at one end of a football field, your dog, from the other end of that football field, would likely either not recognize you, or not see you at all. And our color perception is better than theirs. I am happy to report that a fallacy I believed in my childhood has recently been proven wrong: dogs don't see just black, white, and gray! Studies have shown evidence to suggest that dogs see purple-blues and orange-yellows, as well and black, white and gray. So mostly, they don't see reds and greens (much like human red-green blindness).

One last fact about dogs before we move on to the meat of the book: dogs do not generalize well. There is little value from a survival perspective for dogs to lump objects together and label them. Generalization, or stereotyping, is a human trait. We humans are able to look at a bench, a chair, a sofa and a stool, and label them "seats." Dogs are only capable of doing this after they perceive perhaps forty of such things. They do not, while hunting a deer, look at many trees and see a forest. They are busy focusing on one thing: the deer. Everything else is, more or less, an obstacle. It is for this reason that any and all dog training must start with teaching a new skill to a level of accomplishment (an 80% success rate) in many different environments before beginning to add distractions. The best way to teach a new skill is to teach that skill (i.e., "sit") in every room of your house, facing every direction of every room, at different times of the day, and with you placing yourself in different postures, such as sitting on a chair, sitting on the floor, kneeling on the floor, standing, and lying down. Once the dog has learned that the lowest common denominator of that skill (i.e., hand signal) is the stimulus to watch, you can then begin to add distractions. The list of distractions is virtually endless. In short, distractions can be broken down into sound, motion and smell. We will discuss this in much more detail in future chapters.

BASICS IN A BOX (SORT OF)

There are five major ways we can address behavior. Four of them fall within what we call the "Quadrants of Behavior": positive reinforcement, positive punishment, negative reinforcement, negative punishment, and the fifth one, which doesn't seem to fit into the box but is equally important, is extinction. Let's begin with the "positives."

Positive Reinforcement	*Positive Punishment*
Negative Reinforcement	*Negative Punishment*

The Box

Positive reinforcement is anything that follows a behavior that is presented to the dog that the dog perceives as being pleasant, which serves to increase the chances that that behavior will happen again. It could be a smile, a touch, a treat, throwing a ball, or simply a sideways glance. What matters is that the dog perceives it as being fun, good, or valuable.

So how does the concept of positive reinforcement fit in with all those times that my dog lunges at other dogs when I walk him? The simplest explanation is this: your dog is walking on the leash. This means that of your dog's three normal mechanisms for dealing with threats (fight, flight or freeze), one of them has been taken away. That mechanism is "flight." If your dog feels that he can't increase the distance from an uncomfortable situation (his first natural response), his only real recourse is "fight." But dogs don't like to fight, naturally. They are peaceable creatures. So he's going to use the least amount of aggression possible to get the job done. In this case, a simple lunge/ bark might be all that's necessary.

It might make the other dog back away in fear. This is excellent, from your dog's perspective. Now he can relax. But let's say that the next time you're on a walk, your dog comes across a bolder, more confrontational dog. That dog is going to require more of a show to "make him go away." Now your dog's behavior is being positively reinforced by a more forceful show of "aggression." And, so, on it goes.

The dog on the left does not want to hurt the one on the right; he just needs to communicate his need for distance from the other dog, who had been jumping in his face.

In this situation, you don't mean to allow the aggression to happen. You're not *trying* to reinforce aggressive behavior. You just want to take your dog for his walk. You didn't personally reinforce this behavior. Or did you? Let's look at it a little more closely...

What happens when you realize there's another dog in the vicinity? Do you cringe? Do you get that sinking feeling because you know what's about to happen? Do you tighten up on the leash in anticipation of the lunging? Do you hold your breath? What happens when your dog starts his "aggressive" routine? Do you pull back on the leash? Do you yell at your dog? Or do you tell him "it's OK?" Do you try to hold him back physically? Believe it or not, some of these things are reinforcing to your dog. But ALL of them affect change in your dog's behavior. Think about it: every time he sees another dog and he's on his leash, he gets a leash correction. This teaches your dog that there's an association between dogs and pain/discomfort in his neck, or at the very least, that his person becomes very upset when there's another dog nearby. There *must* be a good reason to be leery of those other dogs, then. No wonder he reacts to other dogs!

Well, what about the yelling? Or telling him "it's OK"? Why don't they work? In order to understand what's going on, we need to learn a few more concepts.

We can make our dog's behavior change in three different directions. The **first** is the one we just learned: to *enhance* the behavior through positive reinforcement. That would be something like "it's OK Rover; that doggy's not going to hurt you." While it's clear to us what we mean to say, our dogs don't understand English. But although he doesn't understand the words, the tone is one he's heard before: soothing, encouraging. "Oh," he thinks. "She wants me to keep doing this! Got it!" And so your dog steps up his efforts to drive the other dog away.

The **second** way we could change the behavior is to *diminish* the behavior through the use of positive punishment. **Positive punishment** is anything which follows a behavior which is aversive to the dog and which serves to decrease the chances that that behavior will happen again. So, you think, I'll just yell at him. That'll stop him. Think again. While your dog is barking, he's barely hearing your voice behind him. And he doesn't know what you're saying, but you must be encouraging him. After all, you're the "big guns" behind him. While you think you're punishing him, he thinks your salutations are supporting him. This is, then, positive reinforcement, which enhances the behavior, rather than positive punishment, which diminishes it.

Positive punishment can be effective if it's severe enough. You should only need to use positive punishment one or two times in order to make that behavior go away. There are several problems with this. First, are you willing to deal a severe enough punishment that the dog is unwilling to repeat the crime? Most of us are not; it usually involves fear or pain, and we didn't get a dog so that we can brutalize him. Second, punishing one behavior "successfully" almost always results in the development of other, even less desirable, behaviors.

But the side effects of positive punishment can be even worse. It is important to understand that it is the perception of the *dog*, not the perception of the *human*, which dictates whether something is punishing or not. So you may never actually USE positive punishment, but the dog may perceive something in his environment as being punishing. A dog who is the subject of repeated positive punishment will react in a predictable manner. At first, the dog becomes **anxious**. You may see signs of this anxiety by looking more closely at him. Are his ears moving around a lot, as if to constantly check the direction

Nose licking is a common calming signal. Also note that Sammy's ears are down and back, and that her eyes are wide open with the whites showing (whale eye).

from which sounds are coming? Is he doing a lot of nose licking and yawning?

Does his leg shake? Is the hair standing up on his back? These are his hackles; it is a line of hair that can stand up, and it runs from the base of his neck to the base of his tail. When the fur stands up like this it is called **piloerection**. Their purpose is to make him look bigger and scarier; it's offensive defense. Hackles may stand up any time the dog is aroused, whether excited, happy, scared or angry. Is his tail moving quickly and with short strokes? Are his pupils dilated? Do his eyes look like dinner plates, huge and round? Does he scan his environment more furtively? His footpads may sweat, which you may see if he's standing on blacktop or tile. A dog's perspiration occurs through the tongue and the footpads. He may tremble or appear to be jumpy at seemingly insignificant stimuli, for example, small noises. An anxious dog will be less able to take food, or to eat his meals. He's

Dogs will often yawn as a stress response. This calming signal may be directed internally or at other dogs or people. These dogs, despite being housemates, are stressed by being asked to sit close together.

Here you can see Demon's nervous grimace from two angles. Note that his upper canines are visible, and his commisures are pulled back.

more likely to experience diarrhea. You may also see quivering lips or a nervous grimace, wherein the sides of his mouth are pulled back and the skin has wrinkles. He may have developed a habit of holding a front paw up in the air when he's uncertain or anxious. He may drool from his mouth, or drip from his nose.

If punishment continues, he might start to become **fearful**. In addition to the previously mentioned symptoms, your dog's body language might include a level of panting that is not consistent with the air temperature. His tail will probably be tucked way under his body. He may suddenly shed copiously, urinate or defecate, or even vomit. It is scientific fact that animals lighten their load before running; an animal who is considering this as an option is one who will remove anything from his body to make running easier. A closer look at his mouth might show a grimace, wherein his **commisures** (the sides of the mouth) are tightly drawn back. At first glance, this might appear to be a snarl. However, in a snarl, the dog intends to display his teeth (his best weapon), whereas in a grimace, they are not. A fearful dog's weight rests mostly on his back legs, as if ready to turn and run (the

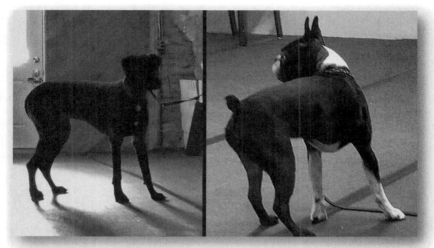

Both Gabe (left) and Opie (right) have their weight on their back legs, as if the are ready to turn and run away. Note Opie's whale eye.

brunt of the weight on a confidently aggressive dog will be on the front legs, so he is ready to pounce).

Fear leads to attempts to **escape** the source of the punishment (you or that particular environment). The dog may go from being only a danger to himself, to being a danger to others because he may try to run away, possibly getting hit by a car. If the dog is inside, he may try to run and hide under a table or a bed, or run to his crate or to the basement. The next level of reactivity to punishment is **avoidance** of the source of punishment altogether. This is where your dog really starts to "blow you off" or runs away from the situation.

Should the punishment continue, the dog may start to show **aggression** as a last ditch effort to get away from the aversive stimulus. This is where you get bitten when you try to get your dog out from under the bed. At this point, the dog feels that he has no other option but to actively protect himself; he is in fear for his life. It is apparent that the dog feels imminently threatened, and is doing anything he can do simply to survive. In dog-human relationships, the dog always loses from here on in. The dog, who has suffered the physical and emotional pain not just of whatever aversive stimulus has followed him, now suffers the physical fallout of stress. Add to this the damaging perception of the human toward the dog as being "stubborn," "vicious," "willful," or "dominant," and most often more punishment follows, not to mention the complete breakdown of any trusting relationship that may have remained between dog and human.

Finally, the dog may give up and display what we call **learned helplessness.** This is where your dog just shuts down. Imagine a dog who just hides under a table, quivering quietly, never willing to come out. The dog rarely eats, cringes when touched, jumps at loud noises, or perhaps doesn't react at all. The dog does not seek out companionship of any human or other animal, may completely avoid eye contact, and is not likely to roll onto his back in a state of relaxation. Tail wagging is more or less nonexistent; his eyes may appear to be vacant. The dog is quite unable to learn new things, and appears to be resigned to a life of mere existence.

It is a fair bet that none of us wants a dog who displays any of the above highlighted terms. It is, after all, a poor definition of the word "pet." While positive punishment may seem to work in the short term, it creates misery in the long term. Not only is it not constructive in teaching a dog new skills with which he can cope with the scary world around him, it also permanently damages the working relationship between you and your dog. Let's just say that we are not going to use positive punishment to help our reactive dogs!

The **third** way we can possibly affect change in our dog's behavior is to **ignore** it. **Extinction** is a very effective tool for changing some behaviors, but one that can be difficult to implement. It means that if some sort of reward does not maintain the dog's behavior, that behavior goes away. The behavior is simply not useful and, therefore, is a waste of energy. For example, if your dog barks to get you to play ball with him, the behavior (of barking) is maintained by your attention (looking at him, telling him he's bothering you and to stop it, and throwing the ball). The more you look at, talk to, admonish him, or throw his ball, the more you are rewarding barking. An example of where this would NOT be the case is when your dog barks at the other dogs walking on the street. Your attention is not likely to play a major role in the maintenance of this behavior. Here, barking most likely serves the purpose of making the other dogs disappear (even though this is superstitious behavior on his part). In this case, extinction would not be the treatment of choice.

If the dog barks at you to get your attention, using extinction would be fairly simple to implement. The barking started because you pick up the ball every time the dog comes to you with the ball. Once in a while you don't take the ball right away, so he barks at you to get your attention. You immediately take the ball and throw it. Throwing the ball reinforces the barking. Now let's say that you are trying to paint your nails or do some other activity which might preclude your throwing the ball immediately. Barking might occur for a little while longer, until you give in and throw the ball. Now the dog has learned to bark all that much longer and, indeed, he'll get the ball thrown for him.

If we put extinction into place here, you will be totally ignoring the behavior of barking. In addition to refraining from taking the ball from him, you are also going to refrain from talking to him, looking at him, giggling at him, yelling at him, stroking him, pushing him away, covering your ears, grimacing, curling up in a ball to get away from the noise, or any other outward behavior which might be construed by the dog as a response to his barking. You are going to see an increase in the duration of time he will bark, the volume of the bark, and you'll probably see him try some other behaviors as well. This is what we call an **extinction burst**. Simply put, it means that the problem will get worse before it gets better. This is where problems arise in implementation. Some people simply cannot ignore the behavior: it's too annoying, or too dangerous. Or it's too risky (barking might get you kicked out of the apartment).

If the purpose of the behavior is to get your attention, and it's not a dangerous behavior, extinction works wonders. You just need to have the resolve to endure the extinction burst. There is a way to help speed the process, too: ignore the behavior you don't like, wait a few seconds, redirect away from that behavior, and reinforce the behavior you do like. Here's an example: your dog whines at you to get some of your popcorn. You ignore it, but ask your dog to target, then sit, and then as a reward you give him a biscuit. So now, you are extinguishing the behavior you don't like, while reinforcing the behavior you do like at the same time! In this case, at least three seconds have elapsed between the whining and the redirected attention; so whining is less likely to be reinforced.

Sometimes the extinguished behavior comes back; this is called **spontaneous remission**. It's a bummer, but if you go through the extinction process again, the progress will be much quicker, and the behavior is usually less intense than the first time it developed. You will usually experience more than one extinction burst, and more than one spontaneous remission in the weeks and months following the extinction of a behavior.

It is important to note that extinction is ineffective if the behavior is self-reinforcing. Licking, if it is not the result of allergies, can be a self-reinforcing behavior, and sometimes, even if it IS the result of allergies, it can develop into a self-reinforcing behavior. Ignoring licking will be ineffective because it's not likely that the dog is licking to get your attention. It's more likely that the dog started licking because of some irritation or due to boredom (self-stimulation). It is important, then, to figure out the motivator of the behavior in order to decide whether extinction will be effective. Self-reinforcing behaviors such as licking, and sometimes barking, can be very difficult to change.

Aside from the two "positives" (positive reinforcement and positive punishment), there are two "negatives" for affecting behavioral change. And as you can imagine, one is less invasive; the other, not so nice. You should start to notice that the word "positive" refers to the addition of something, and the word "negative" refers to the removal of something.

Negative punishment may sound like a bad thing because the word "punishment" is part of the term, but it's really a great way to change behavior! Negative punishment refers to the removal of something that the dog finds valuable in response to a behavior that we want to diminish. Although it sounds confusing, it's actually pretty easy to do. The most important part of it is to figure out what it is that the dog likes at that particular time, and remove it in response to a behavior you want to decrease. For example, if my dog barks at me to throw his ball, I could ignore the behavior (extinction), or I could take the ball and walk away from him (negative punishment). I am the part of the "play ball" equation that he really wants. My walking away from him will, over time, diminish the barking because his barking makes the "good thing" go away. Once he realizes this, the barking will stop. I also want to pair negative punishment with positive reinforcement as much as possible in order to get the best training results. In this case, I'd walk away from the dog, then come back and wait for a minimum of three seconds of quiet before I throw the ball. Negative punishment is my second most valuable training tool behind positive reinforcement.

Negative reinforcement is a little more difficult to fathom. Here, a behavior is increased through the removal of an unpleasant stimulus. In this situation, the dog behaves in a certain way in order to avoid something unpleasant. A good example of this is the manner in which a choke chain is used. When heeling with a dog on a choke chain, the dog is not usually heeling because he finds it fun; rather, he's heeling, or staying right next to you, in order to avoid a correction on the choke chain. If he pulls ahead of you, you might yank on the collar, which is not very comfortable. Once he's experienced this enough times, he will remember this, and try hard to stay within the acceptable boundaries so that he doesn't feel that uncomfortable sensation, and the negative emotional and pheromonal tension that goes along with it. While it doesn't sound like too bad a principle to follow, there is quite a bit of stress involved in this type of reinforcement. This is generally not a wise training approach to follow for a reactive dog, and we'll see why later.

Much of our society works on the principle of negative reinforcement. Why do you observe the speed limit (or fairly closely, anyway) on a highway? Your discretion of speed is negatively reinforced by the knowledge that there might be a police car sitting around the next bend, waiting for speeders. You drive at the speed limit, or near it, to avoid the speeding ticket and the humiliation of being pulled over. [1]

STRESS PUPPY

So…how DO we help our dog?

Hold on tight…we'll get to that…but first we need to understand a little bit about physiological responses to stimuli in the world around us. That goes for both humans and canines.

Let's say that you are driving and have a near-accident. Whew! That was close! But now your **adrenaline** (also known as **epinephrine**) is pumping through your system. You feel shaky, jumpy, and perhaps a little queasy. In about 20 minutes that icky feeling will go away, but in its place your body will produce **glucocorticoids** (we'll call them **stress hormones**) that will remain in your body for up to several hours (durations vary according to the expert you consult). They are produced by your Sympathetic Nervous System in your adrenal glands. The Sympathetic Nervous System is the "all systems go" system, responsible for vigilance, arousal and mobilization. The main purpose of those stress hormones is to put the proverbial "eyes in the back of your head," so you can see that next near-miss coming. As each day goes by, and it seems that you are farther from the possibility of that "Bad Thing" happening again (this is pure survival instinct), those hormones dissipate.

But the day after that first near-accident, you actually see an accident happen some distance away. BAM! There goes that adrenaline again… and more stress hormones are produced. And another two to seven days on top of the first bunch of days. Now you're starting to jump at the sound of a backfiring car, or the rumble of a truck on a distant highway. You seem to be jumpier than normal. Welcome to the world of stress hormones! But after about five days more, you are feeling much better…until a bird flies into your bay window. BAM! More adrenaline, and more stress hormones. Now you are heading toward chronic stress. Every little thing sets you off. You feel like you are constantly on alert. It is off-putting and exhausting. [2]

This is life for some of our dogs. They can't seem to find a calm moment. Some of this is unfortunate circumstance. Some of it is genetics. Some of it is reinforcement history. Some of it is nutrition, health, or inappropriate exercise. Whatever the reason, you, as "benevolent leader," can make a humongous difference in your dog's life. The first thing you need to do is to keep your dog calm for a minimum of one whole week. The longer your dog has been experiencing chronic stress, the longer this "vacation" should be. This gives time for some of the stress hormones to dissipate from your dog's system and allows the **Parasympathetic Nervous System** to take over. The Parasympathetic Nervous System is the opposite of the Sympathetic Nervous System and is responsible for healing, digestion, growth, energy storage, and calm, meditative activities.[2] Keep him home, but take him for long walks in quiet places. Don't take him to pet food stores or dog parks or to places where there's tons of excitement. Just for a week to start. This is going to give him a head start in his ability to learn new habits.

When stress levels are high, learning is low. When a dog is excited or **aroused** (you can call it angry, upset, aggressive, really happy, anxious, scared, or whatever description you choose to use), it is more difficult for the dog to learn anything new. When a dog is very aroused, his ability to take food also decreases. For this reason, we use food as a barometer in the training of a reactive dog. If your dog is not able to take food, he's too aroused. This is going to be a vital indicator for you to use in training your dog, and this information will tell you that you need to change something in your training environment at that time.

And while we're at it, let's refrain from labeling your dog as much as possible. It's not that he's "blowing you off" or "being stubborn" and not taking your food; it's that he CAN'T take the food because he's too aroused! This is a physiological response, not a head game. We need to break away from ascribing negative characteristics to our dogs when they engage in behaviors we don't like. This type of labeling has no place in the interactions with a reactive dog (or any dog, for that matter) because the pheromones you produce and the body language you exhibit when you think such thoughts are obvious

to the dog, if not to yourself. In response, the dog may be less likely
to pay attention to you in an attempt to display calming signals to you.
Thus, the dog may appear to be even more "stubborn" or "willful"
than before. Try real hard to take a step back and look at some of his
behaviors objectively.

RUN IT OFF

Keeping your dog calm does not preclude exercise!

Many of my students complain to me of their dogs' rambunctious
behavior. The dogs chew, jump, pull, dig, nip and bark. They steal
clothing, eat the linoleum flooring, rip the curtains off the walls,
and generally wreak havoc in the home. Why? The answer, almost
unequivocally, is that the dogs do not receive enough exercise (or
management or training)! Most of the time, we are dealing with
adolescent dogs. When they ask me how much exercise their dogs
should get, I tell them what I give my dogs each day. I walk between
two and five miles per day, every day, regardless of weather. My dogs,
however, are off-leash for almost all of that time, so I "guesstimate"
that they do four to ten miles per day!

In all fairness, most folks don't have the dedication to their dogs
that I have to mine (never mind that as an adult I got my first dog so
that I would be forced to walk in the −40 degree temperatures of the
Canadian winter!). Most of them look mournfully or disdainfully at
me when I tell them how much exercise my dogs get. And my dogs
aren't adolescents, either! At this writing, they are 5 and 13 years old.
Most dog owners either won't make the time or simply don't have
the time to walk twice per day for 45 minutes. I wish like crazy they
would, though, because we'd all be healthier!

However, it is very important to recognize that there is more to
exercising a dog than walking. And relatively few people own a
dog who is well behaved and trustworthy enough to be off-leash.
The solution, in my opinion, to effectively exercising your dog is to
engage him in at least two different activities per day. Leash walking
in the neighborhood is a different form of exercise than running on a
wooded trail. Playing tug is form of exercise that uses more muscles
in your body than you knew you had! (It's also good for the dog's
muscles.) Throwing a tennis ball in the backyard is a wonderful way

to burn off excess energy in your dog. But if the weather is horrible, how about throwing that ball down the hallway, or even down the stairs? He'll have to run down, get the ball, and bring it back up for you to throw it again! Even tussling with a squeaky toy provides your dog the chance to burn off energy. If your dog is not trustworthy (and I would imagine that's the case, or you wouldn't be reading this book) but you want to allow him to run around in the local soccer field, buy a long line (a leash which is 20, 30, even 50 feet long) and use that. Most neighborhoods have tennis courts or basketball courts with fencing around them. Sometimes these are off limits to dogs, but if you are careful to use them when other people aren't around (perhaps early morning or late evening) and you are faithful in your doggy doo pick-up, you may be able to get away with using it for some exercise.

If the weather is all-out horrendous or if it's late in the evening and you don't wish to leave the house, play some hide-and-seek. Either have one person hold the dog by the collar while others run and hide (behind doors, in the shower, under the bed, in the closet) in different places of the house, or throw a treat on the floor to distract him while you run and hide. Then call his name happily a few times, and let him sniff you out! Deliver lots of praise and body rubs when he finds you, and then do it again a few more times. While this is not the same as running for three miles, it burns off some energy, allows your dog to use his nose—a valuable sense which we humans ignore, and it ends in fun.

Another version of hide-and-seek involves having your dog find treats instead of you. Have your dog sit stay in the kitchen while you "hide" treats throughout the house (or just that floor of the house). Then come back and tell him to go find them. At first, place them in easily-located, nearby spots. Then later make them a bit tougher to spot so your dog has to start sniffing them out. I used to play this game with five treats when I had one dog, but with multiple dogs I use many and uncounted treats.

A great way to incorporate your dog's dinner with exercise is to broadcast some or all of his serving of kibble in the fenced-in back yard. At first, show him a few pieces of kibble and drop them on the ground in front of him. Help him to find them, and then repeat this several times, tossing the kibble farther away each time. Once the dog learns the "game," you can feed him part or all of his meal in this manner. This activity utilizes a dog's eyes, nose, mouth and total body, and when he is finished, he's likely to lie down and rest! It's great because it encourages his head to be lowered, which helps him to be calm. It also gives him a meaningful job to do—one similar to what he'd do if he were on his own.

In the future, you may be able to ride your bike and have your dog trot slowly along next to you. Some dogs love this and others don't. This activity is one I mention last because there are many aspects to it that may not lend themselves to your dog. Some dogs are too fearful, while some are too excitable or distractible. Some dog owners live in areas with roads which are far too busy, and therefore, dangerous.

Suffice it to say, selecting a minimum of two of these activities per day will be of great benefit to you and to your dog. Exercise is the best way to dissipate the glucocorticoids that your dog has been accumulating. Sustained exercise (trotting along) is more effective than quick bursts of exercise. But any exercise is better than none at all. If you would like to see improvement in your dog, find a way to exercise your dog for 30-45 minutes twice per day or more. My clients with the poorest record of improvement have been the ones who will not find a way to help their dogs to burn off that energy. To me, it is very sad, and completely avoidable.

VET ON IT

I would be remiss if I were to write any more on the topic of reactivity without recommending that any dog who exhibits signs of reactivity visit his veterinarian. While reactivity often is the result of genetics, reinforcement history, stress in the environment, early socialization and other factors, there are many dogs who become reactive in response to a medical issue. Have your veterinarian do a complete medical exam on your dog. Some vets don't check every body part in a general physical exam, so you may have to ask. Vets are good at checking ears, eyes, mouth, nose, pulse and stool, but you may wish to ask for a urine sample, CBC (Complete Blood Count), or thyroid, or have other laboratory tests completed to help you and your vet get a clearer picture of your dog's health. Some issues are well hidden and require lots of detective work to uncover them. Do not hesitate to change vets or get a second opinion if your vet is less than completely supportive and cooperative.

I had a student whose Viszla became reactive as a result of a series of medical procedures. He was diagnosed and treated for a connective tissue injury, and when he didn't recuperate fully post-surgery, he went back for more tests. The prescription for treatment was forced activity, despite resistance from the dog. When the dog began wincing and limping when walking, and then finally growling and showing other signs of fear and aggression, the owner took him to another vet who diagnosed a staph infection. Once that was treated, the dog made a full recovery physically, but was a mess emotionally. Fortunately, we made some lovely progress with him, and he is now a demo dog for basic obedience classes!

Folks who have the frustration, embarrassment and heartache of owning, living with, dealing with, and being associated with a reactive dog need to have a support system in place. One member of that support network should be a veterinarian. There simply is no reason for a veterinarian to show less than complete support in that dog owner's efforts to address the reactivity issue. While some of these tests and vet visits may further increase your dog's reactivity in the short term, they are important enough in the treatment of your reactive dog that it is worth the added stress for him and for you. Then, once you have your results, and if you need some form of medical treatment (drops for an ear infection, thyroid replacement, antibiotics for a urinary tract infection, etc), testing later on will be easier because by then the dog will have learned new skills to allow him to cope with the vet visits later on.

BRUSSELS SPROUT OR BICYCLE

In this next section, we will be addressing what to do with your dog while he is on "vacation." These are the new skills and behaviors he and you will develop at home which will eventually be useful in the "real world."

OK! *Now* we can start to DO stuff with our dog!! Let's start using the concept of **positive reinforcement.** And we'll keep it real simple...*pick out the things your dog does (behavior) that you like, and reinforce them.* There are two main components to that sentence. The first component is to *pick out the things that your dog does that you like.* Do you like barking, growling, shaking, pulling, or lunging? No. So don't reinforce them. We *do* like quiet (no barking or whining), sitting, looking at us, laying down, chewing a bone, or finger targeting. So reinforce them, and only them. These things can be called, "criteria." These will be the things that we will be looking for in our dogs.

The second part of that sentence is **reinforcement** (here we go again!). In order to be able to be effective in our training, we must understand that there are two main types of reinforcers: primary and secondary.

A **primary reinforcer** is one that is necessary for survival, such as food, water, warmth, shelter, sex, air, and interaction (to some extent). This makes it a powerful motivator. But most of these are either too difficult to use or unethical to use. Withholding any of these things might be considered abusive, and providing more of some of them is impossible (for example, air). Obviously, food is the easiest of these to use. It also allows us to do many repetitions, which results in faster skill achievement. Still, the choice of *which* food to use must be selected carefully. Sometimes kibble is exciting...like when your dog

The easiest primary reinforcers to use with dogs are meat-based, smelly foods, such as cheese, hot dogs, doggy salami, and peanut butter.

hasn't eaten in two days. But how interesting is kibble when there's a squirrel nearby, or another dog? Forget the kibble! Whatever that food is, it *must* be more interesting to your dog than the squirrel or the other dog! Sometimes this is impossible…but usually we can get the dog's attention with something really stinky…like cheese, chicken, liver, steak, or tuna. Using a smelly food that is mostly protein in content is your best bet. It is critical for you to find a selection of food treats that your dog finds interesting, even in high-distraction situations.

Then there are **secondary, or conditioned reinforcers**. These are things that have become rewarding to the dog through association with primary reinforcers. For example, being petted by you is not necessarily rewarding to your dog. But we can help it to be rewarding through association with food. Humans value money, but money is a secondary reinforcer because it's not inherently rewarding; you're not born understanding the value of money. It's what we get to buy with the money that makes it rewarding. Some dogs find play very rewarding, while some others need to be taught about play, particularly dogs who weren't socialized well to play as young puppies. Looking at you may not be rewarding at all to your dog, and hearing your voice may not be rewarding at all in some circumstances. But we can teach a strong association between those behaviors and primary reinforcers, so that they become very rewarding. It may be quite a surprise to some folks to learn that dogs do not have a genetic component to them which dictates that the human voice is a thing of value.

We must also take context into consideration. When we are working with our dogs, we can use kibble if the dog is hungry and there's nothing else very interesting nearby or in the room in which you are working. But put your dog in your car in the parking lot of a busy park. The following rewards might be valued this way:

<u>On a value scale of 1-10:</u>

Kibble = 2
Squirrel = 9
Another dog = 8
Bicycles = 7
You = 2
Brussels sprout = 1

Somehow, if you want your dog to pay attention to you, you must be more interesting than the highest value (9).

Aha!

Prime rib (marinated with red wine and garlic) = 8.

You + prime rib = 10!

You need to use something of that high a value in order to maintain your dog's interest level. This is critical to remember. And don't forget that movement can be a really fabulous reward…you standing still might be a 2, but you running around might be a 9!

Back to the work at hand…pick out the things your dog is doing that you like and reinforce it. Make the reinforcer a primary one, and make it good. Using a clicker helps to identify for the dog which behavior you are rewarding. A discussion of clicker training occurs on the following pages. If your dog is barking, simply *wait for three seconds of quiet*, and reinforce that. Remember, effective reinforcement follows within a half second of the occurrence of the behavior. So if your dog is barking, reinforcing after three seconds of quiet reinforces quiet, not barking. Don't forget that while we are waiting for the barking to

The opportunity to chase a thrown ball can be a fabulous secondary reinforcer to some dogs, while others may get very excited over a tug toy or frisbee.

stop we are not going to talk to the dog, yell at him, soothe him, touch him, glare at him, pull on his leash, or otherwise acknowledge his existence. We are extinguishing that behavior. We are reinforcing quiet. (It is important to understand that while your dog may not be barking, he may also not be calm. You can look at his body language and glean clues as to his emotional state, such as his tail and ear set, how big and round his eyes are, whether his hackles are up, etc.). More details on how to accomplish this huge feat of rewarding the absence of barking will follow later.

Conscious Or Not

At this point, it is important to understand that we, and our dogs, learn through two different processes. One is called **classical conditioning,** also known as **Pavlovian learning** or **associative learning.** This is not a conscious thought process on the part of the animal. It means that there is an association that develops between two unrelated stimuli or events, and the more this association takes place, the stronger it becomes. For example, you are driving along with the radio on. A song comes on, and it immediately takes you back to your junior year in high school. This was not something you did consciously; rather, it was the number one hit that year so you heard it over and over for weeks at a time. Now, every time you hear that song, you think of your friend Karen and all of the trouble the two of you found. In terms of your dog, let's find another example. Every morning your alarm clock goes off. Your dog wakes up, but you hit the snooze. Nine minutes later the alarm goes off again, and you turn it off and get up. After experiencing this for several weeks or months, your dog becomes classically conditioned to respond only to the second alarm. He's not trying to consciously figure out when to get up; he's just going with what works. We will be doing lots of classical conditioning with our reactive dogs.

Unfortunately, while it seems that dogs need many repetitions of associative learning in order to build a strong association between two events, this may not be the case if one of the events is scary, aversive, or traumatic. For example, it may only take a dog one episode of jumping on the counter and knocking a pile of dishes on the ceramic floor to teach the dog a very negative association between jumping up on the counter and bad things happening. This is pure survival instinct. Dogs do not generalize well. While it may require us to pair positive reinforcement with an item or event many, many times in order for the dog to perceive that new thing as a positive (we'll see an example called "stuff-a-dog" later), a dog may only need one exposure to the car as a puppy with a full stomach to learn that cars make him vomit. From a survival perspective, he was lucky that one time: no use in pushing it again. Next time, he might not survive it. I call this "single-event learning."

Now we come to **operant conditioning.** This **is** a conscious thought process on the part of the dog, and this is the technique that B.F. Skinner made so popular. This is where the dog actively tries to figure out what the rules are to the game; he is figuring out how to get the goodies. Once a dog figures out the rules to the game, he is likely to begin to offer behaviors to see which one might result in getting a treat or a toy.

In the USA, a popular method of using operant conditioning with dogs is through the use of a clicker. The clicker is a piece of metal crimped onto a piece of plastic, and when you press it, it makes a clicking noise. There is no magic to the clicker; it's the association between the noise and the reward that follows it that makes it so wonderful as a conditioned reinforcer to the subject. If you haven't already taught your dog about the clicker, this might be a good time to do so. There are several ways to teach a dog that "click" means "treat." One way is to place a few goodies on the floor. As the dog picks up each treat, click your clicker. (Make sure you keep the clicker away from the dog's ears; a clicker can be painfully loud!). Repeat this activity a bunch of times. I always tell my students that dogs need 40 repetitions of a behavior before they understand it. If you do this several times, a dozen or so treats each time, over a day or two, he'll start to make the connection. This introduction can be particularly helpful for very fearful or sound-sensitive dogs.

Another, more interactive way to initiate the clicker is to teach, "finger targeting," or "point and click." Hold out your finger (no treats in that hand) off to one side of your dog's nose, no higher than your dog's nose level. Once your finger is in place, keep it still and wait for your dog to touch his nose to your finger (orienting response), and then click your clicker and deliver a treat from your other hand. It might take a while for the dog to figure out how to get rewarded (because we can't explain it to him, due to the fact that he doesn't understand spoken language), but once he gets it, it becomes fairly resistant to extinction. It will be his responsibility to move his nose to your finger, not the other way around. This places the task squarely on his shoulders to pay attention and earn good stuff. I don't know who originally said this, and I'm sure it applies to humans as well as to dogs, but I love the saying and use it often: "The more you help your

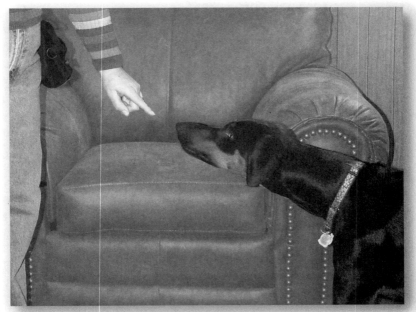

Gerda has learned to touch a finger in order to get a click and treat. Gerda LOVES finger targeting!

dog, the stupider you teach him to be." That means let **him** figure it out!

You may also teach your dog to target to your hand. Hold out the palm of your hand, facing your dog but about six inches away from his face. You will be most effective if your hand or finger is slightly off to the side of the dog's face, as his eyes are set off to the side, not in the front of his face. When the dog touches his nose to the palm of your hand, click and treat. While the dog is thinking and figuring it all out, stay quiet. Save your verbalizations for praise after you click and while you treat. Talking to your dog while he is working will, at best, distract him and at worst, confuse him. In addition, you want to look at your finger or hand, not at your dog. Remember, dogs are masters of body language. If he is at all confused (which he will be), he will look to you for clues.

Once your dog is touching your finger or hand consistently, you want to start adding a word to the behavior. I use "here" for finger targeting and "touch" for hand targeting, but you can use whatever

Hand targeting is another version of finger targeting, and it allows for the owner to create a larger, more obvious target for the dog.

word you choose. Once your dog is pushing your finger or hand like a button, you know he's got the idea. Try for an 80% success rate over several training sessions. At this point, you want to label the word. That means you say the word simultaneously to the nose touch, then click and treat. Do this for about a week (or at least several days) and then you can start to use it as a cue.

If you don't have access to a clicker, or if you find it too confusing to hold a clicker and a leash and treats, or if you feel you don't have the coordination to use a clicker, you may use a **verbal marker**. This is a spoken word of one or two syllables that you say at the very moment the dog does something you like, and which is followed immediately by a treat. Examples of good verbal markers are "Super," "Yay," "Bravo," and "Perfect." Try to use a word that isn't used much in the English language, but that you will easily remember. Some words don't roll off the tongue very nicely and should be avoided. A word in a different language is often a good choice because it is not heard much.

The benefit to using a verbal marker is that you can take it anywhere. The disadvantages to it are several. You need to use a word with the same intonation every time, which can be difficult to remember to do. Humans are a very emotional species, and even if we think we are "acting happy," we might be coming across as irritated or nervous or tired or scared. So using a verbal marker requires some practice to sound like a broken record! The next main disadvantage to using a verbal marker is related to the fact that we humans talk all day long. Blah. Blah. Blah. Somewhere in there, our dog needs to distinguish his name and any possible cues that we may have taught him in the past. That's a very high expectation for a species that is not given to verbal language. And the third main disadvantage is that the word we choose may well be something that other people use frequently. For example, you'd be wise to stay away from words such as, "Good Boy," "Good Girl," "Good Dog," "Yes," and "OK." Imagine your dog jumping up on a visitor, or growling at someone, and that person is saying, "OK, be a Good Boy now. Get down. Yes, that's a Good Boy!" The visitor doesn't know it but he's rewarding that behavior (especially if he's holding his hands out to the dog in trying to prevent the jumping, since many dogs read that body language as an invitation to play!)

Having said all of that, the clicker is not a permanent tool, but rather one that is useful for teaching new behaviors. Once the behavior is learned (the definition of learning that I use is successful completion 80% of the time), it must be successful in different and distracting environments. While the distraction work is being done, the clicker can be replaced with the verbal marker at home, but the clicker should continue to be used in the distracting environment. Only when the dog is able to perform the skill in five or six new environments at an 80% success rate should the clicker be replaced with the verbal marker.

While we are on the topic of clicker training, I feel that it is important to provide a crash course in **free-shaping**. This is training at its most fun and effortless. Free-shaping is the ultimate in clicker training. In this scene, we teach a new skill by **shaping**, or rewarding, successive approximations to the desired behavior. Simply put, we click the dog for offering behaviors we like. There is no luring or talking or physically touching the dog. It's just click and treat.

Start with a very simple behavior. Have your dog sit in front of you. Have your clicker in one hand and treats in the other. Watch your dog without saying anything and without much movement on your part. At some point, your dog will move his head. It might be a glance left or right, or he may look down or (less likely) up. The motion might be tiny and inconspicuous, but click it anyway, and treat. The first bunch of times you do this, he's likely to be confused and maybe frustrated. That's OK. Don't say anything to him other than a little praise after each click. Deliver the treat either to his mouth or toss it on the floor. Your dog probably didn't realize he was moving his head, and if he did, he may also have moved something else as well. Through repetition, he will tease out which behaviors you want and which you don't. After a while, your dog will start to move his head in that same direction as an offering to get a reward, and look immediately back at you. That's the "light bulb moment!" The goal of this activity is simply to teach your dog to *offer* you behaviors. It maximizes your dog's attention toward you, and really builds that working relationship.

Make each of these sessions short, and end them with lots of motion-based fun (run around, play tug or throw a toy). If you and your dog love these sessions, do one behavior and then place yourself either in another room or in another posture (sitting vs. standing), so your dog learns to distinguish that this is a new game. Once the dog is offering a behavior strongly, you can start to associate a word for a while, and then start using it as a command.

This is just an example of a simple behavior, and it is intended to introduce the concept of free-shaping. But this technique is a fun and tremendously successful way to teach complex behaviors. You'll want to teach a 2- or 3-step behavior before you teach something really complex like, "roll yourself up in a blanket." An example of a 2- or 3-step behavior might be, "head down." To do this, start by sitting or standing in front of your dog. Wait for him to sit. Click and treat (place the treat in his mouth this time). Wait again, and the dog will eventually offer you a down. Click and treat your dog, placing the treat on the floor, in between your dog's front paws (remember, dogs migrate to the spot of reinforcement). Now wait again. Eventually, over a number of repetitions, he will lower, and then put his head down on his paws. Click and jackpot! Have a party! Your dog's got it! Now move yourself to another spot in the room in which you are working. Repeat the process, and then repeat it in several different locations, over several days, or at least several different training sessions. When your dog becomes fluent in offering this behavior, label it ("head down," or "are you sad?" or "sorry"). The word or phrase you use doesn't matter, so long as it doesn't sound close to any other cue you've taught.

There are many times that I just do free-shaping for the heck of it. I don't really want to teach my dog any new tricks. She just annoys me to do work, and she's a free-shaping fanatic! So there are times when I'll just sit down and wait for her to offer behaviors (yes, I know, I'm rewarding pestering - naughty trainer!). My input is minimal, and she does most of the work. I often don't label these behaviors, but she enjoys the work and she's calm afterward. We both end up satisfied, and once in a while, she comes up with a really cute or funny behavior that I decide that I want to keep, so I do put it on cue. It *is* the ultimate in a working relationship, in my opinion. It bears mentioning that most trainers will agree that it is best to put new behaviors on cue; otherwise they will be offered at the most inappropriate times!

It is through the use of both controlled classical conditioning and operant conditioning that we can effect positive change in our dogs. Most things that we do to our dogs effect change in them; we need to be careful about what we are changing and how we are changing it. For the most part, we want to ignore the stuff we don't like while paying positive attention to the things we do like (operant conditioning). At the same time, we want to change the underlying emotion in our dogs with regard to certain stimuli (classical conditioning).

You may be wondering why we are discussing teaching tricks when all you really want is to "fix" your reactive dog. The answer is that we are taking some time now to lay a foundation of behaviors based on trust, calm, and working together to have fun, and focusing. Through this process, you will teach your dog some cool new tricks (or, he may teach them to you!) and you'll be able to use them to your benefit when you begin to work with him in the environment in which he needs your help and leadership. You'll be reading more about this in the section entitled, "How's Tricks?"

ARE YOU MY FRIEND?

Dogs are absolute masters of body language. While humans believe they are terrific at spoken, or verbal language, we can't even approach a dog's ability to read the body postures and motions of other animals. It is in their interest as a survival tactic not only to be able to read body language, but also to maintain peace among each other to the greatest extent possible. There is a set of body postures and behaviors in which dogs engage that serve as very concise and important communication to other animals. These behaviors and postures generally say three things: "I'm not being confrontational; I'm your friend," "You seem to be nervous or aroused, so let me calm you down," and/or "I'm nervous and uncomfortable and I need to calm myself down."

If you watch two dogs approach each other, you will not likely see them approach face to face. You will see them curve around each other, and sniff the flews (sides of the mouth), ears, and urogenital area. These are the three areas that impart the most information about a dog because of scent glands located there. Walking in a curved approach is one example of what we call a "calming signal." The term "calming signals" was created as a concept by a trainer in Norway whose name is Turid Rugaas.[3] She has spent many years studying canine body language. Other examples of calming signals include, but are not limited to, sniffing the ground, pawing at the ground, licking the nose, yawning, stretching into a play bow, averting eye contact, turning the head away, turning the body away, freezing, walking or moving slowly, and sitting or lying down. I have also seen dogs lick or scratch themselves as a way of getting the same message across; usually these dogs are trying to calm themselves down. The message in these attempts is one of peaceful coexistence. It can be used as a prevention or as an intervention. Black dogs and black-faced dogs appear to be more apt to use licking, because their eyes and facial expressions are more difficult to see. (If your dog is reactive to other dogs, he's likely to have the most difficulty with black-faced dogs for this reason.)

You may notice that when you call your dog or ask him to do something that he doesn't want to do, he might suddenly become interested in something far off in the distance, or on the ground. These could be calming signals. He might be saying, "I'm not sure I want to do that because the last time I came to you it resulted in something less fun than what I was originally doing." Avoiding your gaze is an easy calming signal to detect. If you are teaching your dog a new skill and he's not sure about it, he's likely to look away from you. It is *not* natural for dogs to make friendly direct eye contact, yet this is one of the first and most important skills we teach our dogs. We are really working away from natural instinct when we do this. No wonder focus can be so difficult to achieve in the face of distractions!

As soon as your reactive dog becomes nervous about something in his environment, his ability to focus on you decreases significantly. He might be exhibiting calming signals but we would rather have him pay attention to us instead. However, it could be worse. Some dogs seem to have had calming signals bred out of them, or have developed very poor use of calming signals. American pit bull terriers,

Sage (left) and Jaxson (right) got too close and they made eye contact. Note their confrontational body language; also note Sammy (background), who continues to focus on Jen, despite the ruckus.

American bulldogs, Chows and Akitas are examples of this first group of dogs. As a matter of fact, bull breeds in general have a much more confrontational appearance than most other breeds. This means that when they see another dog approach, they are more likely than other dogs to give a full frontal stare.

This is an example of a closed mouth full frontal stare, It indicates a transition from calm toward more serious arousal.

This is perceived as confrontational to the other dog, and a fight may ensue. When pit bulls are bred for fighting, calming signals are a very undesirable trait. It is questionable whether the breeders of these dogs are aware of this concept, but selective breeding has managed to achieve its goal just the same. This is not to say that we can't teach more appropriate body language to such breeds. Training can achieve a lot of wonderful results. An orphan pup or a pup who was separated from his littermates way too early is another example of a dog who may have poorly developed calming signals. The best time for a pup to go to his human home is 9 weeks of age. When a pup is sent to his new home at 5, 6 or 7 weeks, he loses out on the opportunity to learn effective use of calming signals with and from his littermates and his mother. He also loses out on the opportunity to learn preliminary bite inhibition, or how hard he can bite in play before it actually hurts the playmate. The continuation of this learning must occur after the pup goes to his new human home and plays with neighborhood dogs or goes to puppy class for socialization. Most of a puppy's prime socialization window occurs before the age of four months.

It is important to start noticing your dog's calming signals. Sometimes it is difficult to decide whether that sniffing is simply sniffing a new exciting spot or if it is a way of telling you that he is nervous. Generally speaking, if you and your dog go to a new place, exploratory sniffing should be expected. If your dog is sniffing the ground right outside your back door when you are trying to work with him, he's likely using calming signals. Once you start to get an idea of your dog's body vocabulary, you will be better able to understand when an environment is too difficult for him. If he is using calming signals he is not likely looking at you, and you can't communicate with him. The result should be that you remove him from that immediate environment to a safer, less threatening or stimulating one, and wait for the dog to become calm enough in that safe environment so that you can get eye contact or finger targeting from him, for which you can reward him. Now, finally, you are on the road to being able to redirect your dog away from over-stimulation!

Opie is very uncertain of his situation. Mary Beth needs to get his focus or get him out of the situation.

Sometimes this is a means to an end (the end being that the dog learns that the world isn't so scary after all, and can be calm and attentive to you while checking out his world) and sometimes this is the best you can get. For the latter dogs, we must be just a bit more diligent. We have to be on the lookout for the signals our dogs give us when they are nervous, and manage their world by either not putting our dogs in situations which we know will create stress, and/or by continuing to learn which environments create that stress, redirect the dog away from the "scary" thing, get his focus back to you, reward him and put him in a safer place. For most of us, this is a process and we fall somewhere within this range.

STRIKE A POSE

Let's look for a moment at *your* body language. Since body language is, for the most part, how dogs communicate most effectively, what we say with our bodies can really make a difference to our dogs. While we may think nothing of how we stand, on which leg we lean, or where we place our hands, these may indicate strong messages to our canine pals. Earlier, I mentioned that eye contact is not a natural friendly behavior for dogs because it is perceived as confrontation. The reality is that there are many more elements of our body posture that send signals. I am not implying here that our dogs think we are dogs, but our body language does cross species lines. Examples of these include hovering over your dog, bending forward at the waist, placing your hands on your hips, crossing your arms in front of you, standing directly facing your dog, staring at your dog, and reaching out to pat your dog on the head.

Let's look at each one of these in turn. Hovering over your dog is akin to the action of another dog placing his paw or chin on the back of your dog. The message is, "I'm in charge here." While this may be true, as we have been working on teaching your dog that you are "benevolent leader," the behavior of hovering over your dog is every bit as confrontational as someone coming up behind you and squeezing the back of your neck. We tend to hover over our dogs when we are petting them, putting on their leashes, or trying to teach them to sit or lie down. Our intention is not to be confrontational, but many people have been bitten simply because they leaned over a dog.

With your reactive dog, the less confrontation and anxiety we cause for him, the more quickly he'll be able to learn.

The same is true for bending over at the waist. Instead of hovering or bending at the waist, try standing sideways to your dog (shoulder facing him) or bending at the knee. These postures are much more dog friendly. If you are teaching new skills such as sit, down, or stand, you will need to teach them with your body in a sitting or kneeling posture, but then you will have to teach your dog to generalize the verbal and/or hand signal to when you are standing erect.

Placing your hands on your hips, crossing your arms in front of you, and standing directly facing your dog, and staring at your dog all mimic postures of an extremely confrontational dog. Remember the discussion of some of the bull breeds? A dog whose intent is less than friendly, whether it is to warn off an intruder or protect his

Non-confrontational body language includes standing sideways to your dog, arms down or behind your back, and standing in an erect but relaxed posture.

mate/litter/pack, will stand directly facing and staring at the other dog. His hackles may go up, his tail may go up, and his chest may puff out so as to look as large as possible. Placing your hands on your hips and standing directly facing your dog make you appear to be large and confrontational, while crossing your arms in front of you may make your chest look puffed out. Again, standing sideways will diminish this message. Cocking your head a bit, looking out from an angle of your eye as opposed to straight out the middle of your eye, or keeping

Mary Beth's body is not directly facing Opie's; her weight is not balanced, and her head is slightly angled.

your chin at a 45 degree angle to the ground so that your eyes are soft, may also help calm your dog.

Reaching out to pat your dog on the head is another biggie. This action places your dog in a position of losing one of his senses: vision. A dog who is nervous about the world around him feels a desperate need to know what is going on. Blocking his vision, especially his view of someone who is approaching him, puts him in a compromised position. Sure, we try to keep the dog calm and quiet as much as possible by putting him in his crate when we're not doing activities with him, but when we are working with the dog, we want him to learn that while he can check things out, he needs to check back in with us every few seconds. By blocking one of his senses, we increase his anxiety, and that, we know, decreases the ability to focus and learn. His normal response would be to back away and avoid the hand; in extreme cases, that hand might get snapped at or bitten. A simple

Acacia strongly dislikes being touched on the top of her head.
She will duck away, or back away. This particular time, she
swivelled her head in an upward manner.

alternative to reaching over a dog's head is to pet the dog on the cheek or under the throat.

These tips are very important to remember when other people are interacting with your reactive dog. While these postures may not have such an obvious effect coming from you, they are certain to have a substantial effect if they are coming from someone less familiar.

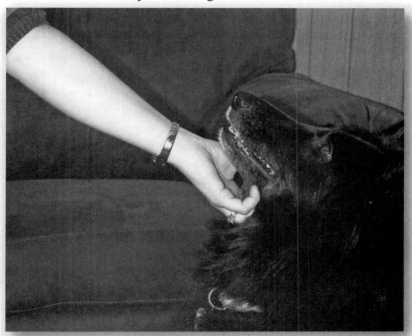

Acacia loves to be scratched under the chin. (Must be all the hair!)

IN THE PHYSICAL REALM

YOU ARE WHAT YOU EAT

We've all heard that saying. How true is it? Let's explore the meaning of this concept with regard to our dogs.

Dogs are omnivores, like us. That means that we thrive on a variety of fare. Dogs will eat meat, fat, berries, grasses, and to some degree, carrion. Dogs are opportunists. Noted author and professor of biology Ray Coppinger and his wife Lorna theorize that we didn't domesticate dogs so much as dogs domesticated themselves [4]. I tend to believe this theory. Certain subsets of wolves began to realize that they derived some benefit from hanging around human settlements. Humans are wasteful, and throw away food. Wolves can eat and survive on this food. Over time, and in many simultaneous locations worldwide, some wolves became less fearful of human activity and benefited from it. This was the beginning of the dog. What foods were they eating? In general, they ate meat, bones, and leftovers.

Centuries into this process, humans began to purposefully keep dogs with them and near them. We began to selectively breed them to enhance some of their natural characteristics to suit our needs. Much of the time, we left them to fend for themselves. Sometimes we supplemented their diets with our leftovers and offal from our killings. Their diets varied in accordance with the environment in which they lived.

It was only in the 20th century that dogs started to eat grains and prepared foods. Food processing companies realized that there was actually a market for their leftovers, and the commercial dog food market was born. Much of the basis for this food was grains. Added to this were leftover meats. It seemed that we really catered to our pets and assistants. They never had it better. Or did they?

It turns out that dogs don't need grains. As a matter of fact, they only digest grains at a rate of about 55%. They digest meats at a rate of about 80-85%. Dogs have a short digestive tract; what goes in gets processed rather quickly. Humans, on the other hand, have a long and reticulated digestive tract. That which enters the human body completes a long and tortuous path. There is much time for things to go wrong and foods to become rancid in the human body, and there are many crevices in which food can become lodged.

While on first inspection it would seem that grains don't pose much of an issue at all, on a closer look, we realize that they have the potential to wreak havoc on the canine body. Grains are not very digestible; so much of it is simply excreted. But that means that the dog needs to eat more food to get sufficient nutrition. That means more stool and more shedding, and poorer coat and skin. For some people, this is not much of a concern. But take a good look at any of the most popular commercial dog foods, and you'll see that these grains (which are not very digestible) are the second and sometimes the first ingredient in the food. Since ingredient lists must show the ingredients in the order of weight percentage (volume), it suddenly becomes clear that much of the content of these dog foods are poorly digestible or are indigestible. The grains are fillers. They are cheap ingredients and poor sources of protein, often obtained as floor sweepings from grain processing plants.

These grains are billed as being excellent sources of proteins and complex carbohydrates. What these companies don't tell you is that dogs don't need much in the way of carbohydrates. Dogs eat grasses. My dogs especially love the tender shoots of new grasses in the spring; they do not seek out the flowering heads of these grasses. Grains are the seeds of grasses. The wheat and corn that we feed our dogs have no natural place in the world of a dog. These substances do not exist in a natural form. In many cases they have been genetically engineered. Better choices for carbohydrates in commercial dog foods appear to be rice, oats, barley, sweet potato and potato, sorghum, and amaranth.

The lesson to be learned from this discussion is to find a food that has little grain in it. The worst grains are corn and wheat. The reason? These are the most commonly used. Soy is also a top culprit in dog food. It is usually genetically modified, and soy is often planted between other crops in order to fixate nitrogen in the soil. The purpose? To remove toxins from the soil left by other crops. (Organic soy products aren't nearly as insulting an addition to the diet.) They are among the top four food allergens in dogs. Vets and dog professionals all across America hotly debate this issue. But generally speaking, the four top food allergens are corn, wheat, soy and chicken. A food allergy can also be described as food sensitivity. Food sensitivity develops when too much of the same food is consumed repeatedly, with little variation in the diet. When this happens, consumption of that food must be discontinued for a period of time (months, perhaps). Sometimes the food can never be consumed again.

This topic is pertinent to the lives of our reactive dogs because of the manner in which food allergies present. Many dog owners believe that itching is the first sign of an allergy. For sure, dogs can develop red, swollen patches with hair loss. But dogs are also likely to develop behavioral issues. It is possible that these issues are related to the discomfort of itching skin, but they don't always occur together. Food allergic dogs may appear to be irritable, barky, or snappy. It may be more difficult to get and keep their focus, and they may respond more quickly and more intensely to stimuli in their environments. Their threshold level for arousal decreases, and they may bark, growl, snap or bite much more readily than another dog.

It is hard to know why some dogs react poorly to certain foods, while others seem to have no problem. But again, it's the same old story. It's a combination of genetics, environment, stress level, variety and quality of food, among other variables. In many cases, a dog will appear to tolerate a food for years, and then suddenly become intolerant to it. Your best bet in feeding your dog is to feed as much variety of ingredients as possible, and to switch your dog's brand regularly if your dog can tolerate it. This way, your dog will consume many ingredients and will be less likely to develop a sensitivity to any one item.

But the issue of food doesn't stop with allergies. Take a good look at the ingredients in your dog's food. Artificial colors, flavors and preservatives abound. Propylene glycol is a common ingredient in dog foods and especially treats, and yet it is considered to be a toxin by the FDA. What are the sources of the proteins in the food? Often, the animals are the rejects from the human food industry: the maimed, injured and sick animals. As disgusting as it sounds, it is a well-known fact that cancerous parts of cattle are excised in the processing plant and put into some pet foods. Do we really want our dogs to be eating this?

Oils and fats are another main component of dog food. Do you question the words, "animal fat" in your dog's food? What, exactly, does that mean? Which animal does this fat come from? Avoid foods that list vague sources such as this. "Poultry fat" is another one to avoid. Which type of poultry is it? Chicken, duck, turkey, quail, pigeon? In general, animal fats are a poorer choice of fat than vegetable because they don't provide the range or ratio of EFAs (Essential Fatty Acids) necessary to maintain optimal health. At this writing, there is lots of discussion about which vegetable fats are best. Current debates on the potential hazards of soybean oil (and soybeans in general), safflower oil and canola oil cause me enough concern to warn against their use. Sunflower oil, olive oil, and fish body oil (not fish liver oil, because the liver filters toxins out of the animal's body) are some good ones to look for in your dog's food. Remember that fats and meats go rancid easily, so keep your dog's food stored in a cool and dry location.

Consider how the food is prepared. Most dry dog foods are extruded. This means they are cooked very quickly and at very high temperatures. As a result, many to most of the biological nutrients are killed. Substances such as acidophilus are killed in these high temperatures, and these are substances that are beneficial to a dog's intestinal system. There are, however, foods that are baked more slowly, and these appear to retain a more healthy balance of live nutrients.

We should aim to feed the best food we can afford to our dogs, for the same reason we should feed ourselves the best food we can afford for ourselves. We are what we eat. If we eat fast food and pasta and potato chips and candy most of the time, we will survive, but our immune systems and nervous systems will be compromised. Over time, we will get colds and the flu, sinus infections, suffer from seasonal allergies, and eventually even more serious illnesses. We also may suffer from irritability and a short temper because our nervous systems aren't getting the nutrition they need to run smoothly. Better to eat vegetables and fruits, meats and nuts and olive oil. Better still, eat organic foods. The same goes for our dogs.

And then we come to perhaps the most debated of all food issues: feeding raw food. This topic is outside the scope of this book, but I must comment that feeding whole foods in the most natural state possible, and in the correct balance, has shown time and again to have nothing short of a miraculous effect on many a reactive dog. Dogs get biologically appropriate foods rather than fillers, and it affords the savvy owner the opportunity to provide a variety of foods. Many dog owners do not have the time, patience, or knowledge to feed their dogs a raw diet. However, new companies appear regularly which produce ready-made organic frozen raw diets. The work is already done for you. If this concept piques your interest, it is well worth your time to investigate. There are some well-written books out there that delineate a proper feeding routine that will ensure optimal health. Many veterinarians are not fans of this concept, however, and you would do well to find a support group or another knowledgeable raw feeding dog owner to hold your hand for a while!

A CALGON MOMENT

Another set of skills that may help your reactive dog is calming touch. This concept may go by a number of names and titles, but the goal is the same. You want to help your dog to feel as calm as possible before placing him in an environment that may be scary or anxiety producing for him. Several decades ago, Linda Tellington-Jones [5] worked out a series of ways to touch your dog (she began her work with performance horses) that helps to achieve a number of goals. She dubbed the style of calming touch she uses, "TTouch." While at first glance this tactile work looks like massage, it really is calming touch. It increases intercellular communication within the subject being touched, and it increases the trusting bond between you and your dog. It also has the added perk of helping you to feel calmer, too!

One technique that seems to be common to all styles of calming touch is the long body stroke. Start by having both hands on the dog, one stationary and the other moving. It is often easiest to loop your thumb or finger of your stationary hand in your dog's collar. The moving hand starts at the back of the top of the head and goes gently down the back, all the way to the tip of the tail. You'll want to take long, calm breaths while you do this to relax yourself as much as possible, too. At first, your dog may not feel comfortable with this. He may fidget or try to walk away or pull away. Over time, however, dogs usually come to love this procedure. I have introduced this to many dogs who initially struggled with the touch, but after only a few strikes, stopped fussing, let out a big yawn, sat, then laid down, and let out a huge sigh. The owners are always stunned. While you can do this with your dog in any position, your best bet is to try to have your dog lying down. When I do calming touch with my dogs, I like to sit straddled on the floor and have them lying in the crook of my legs. That way I can keep my stationary hand on their chests and be able to move my other hand around easily.

Montana loves the long body strokes. Note that I have a stationary hand on her chest, while the other hand moves.

You want to make sure that you do this sort of thing before you work with your dog, not during a scary moment. This is because you don't want to reinforce fearful or reactive behavior. This is a very easy mistake to make at first, and one that can increase your dog's reactivity. Do a few minutes of calming touch before you take him in the car, or before doing some training with him. Do it before you leave for the vet's office, rather than while in the waiting room. And do some calming touch in the evening, close to bedtime, when everyone's usually kind of dopey, anyway!

Another simple touch to do with your dog is ear-work. It is easiest to do this with your dog in front of you, facing away from you (see photo). Place the knuckle of your forefinger at the inside of the base of an ear, and your thumb on the outside. Stroke outward from the base of the ear to the tip. Repeat this stroke until you've covered the entire ear, then work on the other one. Make sure you have both hands on your dog at the same time, to complete the energy circuit. Your dog is likely to find this a really strange sensation, and may try to walk away from it. Over time, and with gentle perseverance, he will likely learn to tolerate it, and even love it. Once you and your dog are both comfortable with this exercise, you can alternate strokes and ears, or work with both hands on one ear and then the other. Make sure you are stroking gently and without pulling. Your pressure should be

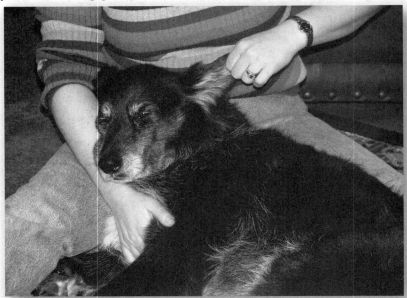

Like the long body strokes, one hand is stationary on the dog while the other hand works on the ear, going in a soft but firm stroke from the base to the tip of the ear. This is a good technique to use in the case of emergencies.

neither too hard nor too soft, and always go from base to tip of ear. Many dogs love to have their ears rubbed, so this activity is often an easy one to incorporate into your dog's routine.

My ability to describe these processes in detail and on paper is poor, so again, I'll recommend that you investigate some books and videos on your local bookstore shelf or online. Overall, the more time you spend calmly touching your dog in a calm environment, the more relaxed he is likely to be, and the more he is likely to trust you. That trust will be critical in the work on which we are about to embark

POTIONS

There are many dog professionals and dog lovers who use and believe in a variety of homeopathic remedies to help their pets deal with anxiety and fear. Your veterinarian may discount many of these because they are not scientifically tested and/or proven to be effective. Some vets may express amusement and tell you it's all a placebo effect. Personally, I believe that if I give my dog something fairly innocuous and it helps me to feel like I'm helping my dog, I don't care whether it's a placebo effect or not! If I feel calmer because of it, and that calm is being communicated to my dog, then I'm being successful! Besides, as a person who tries hard to avoid the use of pharmaceuticals, I'd rather use something natural and/or homeopathic, anyway. In my opinion, it's less poisoning.

One particular substance that I use is the Bach's Flower Essences. These are a series of 38 homeopathic flower and plant essences that are bottled in small vials. Each comes with a metered eyedropper lid. Dr. Edward Bach developed the essences in the early 20th century in England for use in humans, and it expanded for animal use later on. The essences utilize molecular energy resonance and healing. They have little or no actual molecules of the flower or plant named on the bottle (homeopathy maintains that the more dilutions there are, the stronger the effect). The solutions are bottled in a brandy base. They are available at health food stores, and they come with a guide that helps you determine which essence to use. While this guide is designed for humans, entire books have been written on the use of Bach's Flower Essences for pets[6]. You may combine several essences, or use a premixed formula called, "Rescue Remedy." The easiest way to use it is to put two drops in your dog's water bowl each time you refill it.

DAP is a product sold under the trade name, "Comfort Zone." This is synthetically produced Dog Appeasing Pheromone, a pheromone produced by the mother dog that tells her pups to not worry about things in the environment, but to pay attention to her. It has a powerful calming effect in that situation. DAP comes in vials that are used in a plug-in, much like an air freshener. Place the DAP near your dog's crate or bed, and your dog will begin to migrate to that area when he is tired, worried or scared. It usually takes about a week to see changes in your dog. DAP seems to work best for dogs who are fearful of loud noises such as thunderstorms and fireworks.

Essential oils can also be of benefit for anxious dogs. Lavender has long been used for both children and dogs as a calming agent. Simply mix some good quality lavender essential oil with water in a small spray bottle and spray your dog's bedding, crate, or resting area several times per day. I've even sprayed my dogs' butts on occasion!

There are other substances you can give your dog, such as nutritional supplements. These products abound, and new ones come on the market daily. Salmon oil is a particularly useful supplement to add to your dog's food, as it is not only great for skin and coat, it can help to calm agitated nerves. Begin with a small amount and build to a maximum of 10 mg per 10 pounds of body weight. It is possible to spend an inordinate amount of time researching these products; I have listed here the ones my students and I have had success with. In some cases, it's a matter of "Buyer Beware."

THE RIGHT STUFF

All right. We've talked about stress and stressors, classical conditioning, operant conditioning, body language, the "four quadrants of reinforcement" (positive and negative reinforcement, positive and negative punishment), extinction, calming signals, primary vs. secondary reinforcers, food, and calming touch. In this first week, while your dog is having a "vacation," you have learned much about how to effect behavioral change. Except how to change behavior! So let's start building a plan for our reactive friend.

As with any dog (or child, for that matter), the best approach toward dealing with life is to combine **management** and **training**. Let's look at management first, as this is where the critical concept of **safety** lies. Your training efforts will only be as good as your management allows it to be.

Management involves putting your dog in a "safe" place, no matter where he is or what's going on around him. As a responsible dog owner, it is imperative for you to make certain that your dog is safe, regardless of what's happening. If I have my dog in my presence, on leash or off, in the house or out of it, my priority is to ensure his safety. There are endless components to this, so let's look at a few of the main ones.

Crate. Also known as "den," "kennel," "house," "castle," or "space." Canids are den animals. That means that if they are tired or scared, don't feel well, are having puppies, or if they need protection from the elements, they will go into their dens. Domestic dogs aren't likely to dig a hole in a hillside, but the denning instinct is just that, an instinct. So we humans, as benevolent leaders for our pets, give our dogs access to crates to give them security. Ultimately, a crate should be covered on the top, bottom, back and sides, but with the front open so he can see out of it. I like to place my dog's crate in the corner of a room and cover it with a dark-colored, lightweight material on the top and the remaining open side. I leave the very bottom part of that side uncovered so my dog can see me enter the room. The front door of the crate provides my dog the ability to look around. I encourage my students to crate their dogs in their bedrooms. Dogs are social animals. Forcing them to sleep alone may increase their anxiety. Sometimes it is best to have two crates; one for the bedroom and one in a room that is more centrally located relative to the bulk of the activity in the house. You don't want your dog isolated just as much as you don't want him in the middle of the living room. It's way easier to put your dog in a crate in the dining room (in most houses) when an unexpected visitor arrives than it is to take him up to his crate in your bedroom.

Teddy loves his crate because it's where he gets his special Kong toy, stuffed with goodies!

Some training is necessary to teach the dog that this crate is a wonderful place to be. The best way to do this is to start with a very young puppy, if possible. Throw treats into the crate and let the dog go in and get them. Alternatively, you may stuff a Kong® and toss that into the crate. Make no attempt, at first, to close him in. Let him come out and wonder when the next treat is going in, so he can follow it in and eat it. It is best to do little sessions of this over many days, and possibly, weeks. If your dog is, at first, resistant to going into the crate at all, just walk away and let him get his treats on his own time. You may diminish the amount of food he gets at other times during the day to stimulate the interest in the treats in the crate. Remember to use high value treats for this activity. Eventually, your dog may go into the crate and wait for treats. You may even find that he goes in there to nap. This would not be surprising, as it is well understood by many trainers that "Dogs migrate to the spot of reinforcement."

Once this starts to happen, you can close the door, feed several treats through it, and open it again quickly. Gradually lengthen the period of time in which the dog is closed in the crate. Give lots of calm, quiet praise and treats and attention while he is in the crate, and as soon as the crate door opens, he gets no attention whatsoever (for a short time). From here, you can start to walk away from the crate while he's in it. At first, take only one step before you immediately turn around and come back and treat and praise, and then open the door. The dog will figure out that staying in there makes the game go on and good things happen when he's in there. Gradually increase the distance you travel before turning around and going back, but try hard to be unpredictable in how far you travel. Predictable is boring, and a poor training strategy when it comes to distance traveled and rewards given.

Should your dog start to fuss while you are working on this part of his crate training, simply wait for a minimum of three seconds of quiet and calm (absence of barking, whining, scratching, stomping around) before you resume what you were doing. Making noise and fussing makes everything stop. He doesn't get rewards, he doesn't get out, and he doesn't get chastised. So these behaviors will no longer work (think of a two-year old having a tantrum), and they will stop. During the time that your dog is fussing, completely avoid looking at him or talking to him. Any attention at all to this behavior will likely increase it. If you are out of the room when this happens, avoid walking toward the room or the crate. Remember that your dog's ability to hear is very good, and he will interpret your walking toward him as rewarding the fussing. So, simply wait until the fussing stops for three seconds, and *then* walk toward him. Once your dog starts to be quiet and calm for three seconds, increase the expectation to five seconds, then ten seconds. It is at these longer intervals that your dog will start to understand that calm and quiet is the key to gaining access to getting out. He will also start to feel calmer in the crate, and thereby find it more rewarding to be in it.

If your dog has a real aversion to the crate, and going in to get those treats, no matter HOW wonderful they are, is just too scary, there are a few things you can do. One is to put phenomenal treats in the crate and close the door. Your dog will wonder how to get in there to get those goodies—give him an hour or so, then open the door and walk away, letting him go in, without pressure, to get the treats. Repeat a hundred times.

You might also want to **free-shape** going into the crate. If you and your dog have done free-shaping before, and he's "free-shape savvy," the process will take less time than if this is the first time you're trying the process. For this reason, you would be wise to first do some of the free-shaping activities mentioned in the operant conditioning section of this book. When your dog has learned the game of free-shaping, you can work on the following game.

Armed with a clicker and a pile of fantastic little yummies, sit outside the crate. Again, you may want to start this activity with the door completely off the crate if possible. Otherwise, just make sure it's open as wide as possible, and sit on the side opposite to the hinges. You want to avoid the situation where the dog fears he might be pushed in and locked up. Now look at the crate. Wait for your dog to acknowledge its existence, whether it's looking at it, or sniffing it, or touching it accidentally. Click and treat, placing the treat outside the crate. Then look at the crate again. Click and treat at the same level (i.e., the dog looks at the crate) up to five times. There's a good chance he'll try something different in that time, and then you want to click and treat that. But let's say he looks at it five times and you've clicked and treated it each time. The next time, you don't want to reward that behavior. Wait for something better. That slight level of frustration will usually motivate him to try something different and a little more intense. Rewarding the same behavior five times had the effect of building confidence. He learned that that behavior resulted in good things. If, suddenly, it doesn't result in a reward, he'll feel bold enough to try something different, no matter how slight. But an insufficient frequency of rewards at this early and potentially scary level is likely to backfire on you.

Now you've waited for him to, say, touch the crate with his nose, and you click and treat that a bunch of times. Then stop rewarding that, and wait for something better. Perhaps he sticks his head a few inches inside the crate. Remember to always place the treat outside the crate for now. While we usually place the treat where we want him to be, this situation is a little different. First, we don't want to "lure" him into the crate. He is likely to perceive that as pressure, and for a dog in this situation, it will backfire. Second, we want many repetitions of going in and coming out. If you start placing the treat inside too early on, he'll just sit there until the treats stop, and that is not really the behavioral pattern we want to teach. It is more the action of going into the crate that we are shaping.

However, at some point, your dog will go inside the crate, look at you and wait for that click, come out and get the treat, and then run back in and look at you. Once you've rewarded this several times, you will start waiting for him to sit in the crate before you reward, and then lay down. Once you get the laying down behavior, start to increase your duration (how long he lays there) before you reward. Now is the time to start treating him inside the crate for being in there. Use tons of praise, too! Start to close the door (don't latch it yet) and throw lots of treats in there and praise happily. Then open the crate door and walk away, paying no attention to him at all. The next steps from here involve increasing your distance from the crate, and eventually leaving his sight. Once you can leave his sight briefly, then you should start to work on the latching part of the sequence. Latching may be extremely anxiety producing for your dog, so go very slowly on this. And remember, you need to appear to be relaxed and confident in this entire endeavor, or he's not going to believe you or trust you. Make certain that you move with confidence. Try hard to avoid hesitating and tiptoeing around. Know exactly how many steps in which direction you are going to take before you do it.

Most often, your best training tactic is to do lots of little sessions. However, in this case, in addition to using operant conditioning, we are doing a combination of counterconditioning and desensitization. These types of work yield the best results when they are done in longer sessions, so instead of the one to five minute sessions I usually recommend for teaching new skills, crate training might proceed more quickly if you do 10- or 15-minute sessions.

Occasionally, a dog is simply not a good candidate for crating. Usually, this type of dog is one with true separation anxiety. There are many dogs out there with anxious behaviors; this is different than true separation anxiety. If your dog whines, cries, barks, and/ or scratches at the door to be let out, he is experiencing anxiety. If these behaviors are rewarded (by letting him out of the crate), they are likely to increase in intensity, length and duration. A true diagnosis of separation anxiety involves a dog who will break teeth and/or claws to get out, bends the bars on a wire crate, salivates heavily, vomits, urinates and has diarrhea in the crate. The dog is experiencing a panic attack and is a true threat to himself, as he will not stop at anything to get out of the crate, house, or other confined area. Separation anxiety is not easily dealt with, and these dogs may require medication. If you think your dog has separation anxiety, speak with your vet sooner rather than later about it; waiting around will only exacerbate the panic and make treatment more difficult. These dogs should not be crated, but confined safely otherwise.

Other examples of safely confining a dog might include an **exercise pen** (perhaps with a cover over it) or using a **baby gate** to keep a dog in a room such as a kitchen or mudroom. It might even be a good idea to have a crate in that room or that area, but with the door off (a plastic Vari-kennel is the best choice in that case). Some dogs love going into a confined area such as a crate, but react poorly to being enclosed completely. The enclosure (baby-gated kitchen or exercise pen) provides the management against chewing and other destructive behaviors, while the crate provides a sense of coziness. Again, some training may be necessary to teach the dog that this is a safe place. If a dog with separation anxiety fares poorly in these environments, he may need a dog-sitter or doggy daycare to keep him safe

Leash. If I am on one end of the leash and my dog is on the other end of the leash, I had better be paying attention to what's going on at that other end of the leash. It is not appropriate for me to be walking my dog and then stop to talk to someone without understanding that I might need to stop what I'm doing and pay attention to my dog. Some of the worst situations occur with the dog on the leash and the owner holding the leash. If you're not paying attention, it's easy for the dog to pull that leash right out of your hand. If you've been paying attention, this is much less likely to occur. If you've been paying attention, you will likely recognize a situation where you may need to intervene with your dog and his reaction to something in the environment. Then you can prevent a problem, rather than deal with it.

A large part of being an effective dog owner is in understanding the appropriate uses for a leash. A leash is NOT a fishing line. Its purpose is NOT to reel in your dog when he's wandering at the end of it! A leash IS there for protection; it protects your dog from being run over. Let's discuss leash management in a little more detail here.

Many owners have a hard time simply attaching the leash to the dog. The dog either runs away from it or jumps up and down out of excitement. Some dogs mouth their owners' hands. Teaching leash management starts with getting the danged thing on in the first place! Here's how to do that: Make the act of having a leash put on immediately result in getting something good. For some dogs it's a treat. For some, it's getting out the door so they can lift their leg on the nearest tree. Figure out what turns your dog on. Let's take the excited dog and treat example, and then progress to the scared dog, and then the leg-lift example.

Have in hand your leash and a bunch of treats (do this when it's NOT imperative that the dog go out; this is a training session). If you use a clicker, have one of those, too. Stand by the door you wish to use, and wait for your dog to sit. You may be tempted to ask him to sit, but he will learn the expectation much more quickly if he has to figure it out on his own. If you need to, ask him to sit only the first three times, then wait for him to offer it, but only ask once each time! Reward the behavior when it happens. Now start to lean down toward your dog, as if you're going to put the leash on him. If he doesn't move after you've leaned halfway down to the level you intended to get to, reward him. If he jumps up or otherwise misbehaves, simply put the leash down in a place that he can't reach, and walk away. Go do something else for a few seconds or minutes, and then come back and start over. This activity goes on the premise that the dog loves going out on a leash. He will, rather quickly, learn that the only way he gets to go out is if he does something in particular. It might take him a while to figure out precisely what it is that he's supposed to do, but the more concise the timing of your reward, the more effectively you'll be communicating. At some point you will be able to walk to the door, stand and look at your dog, who will immediately sit while you put on the leash. It's time to celebrate!!

Now let's look at the dog who is afraid of the leash. There may be many reasons for this occurrence, but a good behaviorist looks not at

David's dog becomes so excited when he picks up the leash for walk time that he can't get the leash attached to the collar.

the reasons for behavior, but how to change them. Now is the time to use classical conditioning to help build a more positive association with the leash. For this dog, start with a fistful of treats and the leash.

Pick up the leash and throw a treat to the dog. If even this action sends him running, you may need to start carrying the leash around and tossing treats to your dog for a while (hours, days, weeks). Toss the treat behind your dog so he gets to go away from the scary leash as an additional reward. Your dog will eventually associate the leash with good things. While you are doing this, watch your dog's body language. Are his ears back? Does his tail go down between his legs? Your criteria in this situation are for ears to be perky and forward and for his tail to be relaxed, or preferably, wagging. There is no way to know how long this process will take, but you can hedge your bets by using really good food (i.e., a value of 10 on my earlier scale). Once your dog is more relaxed around the leash, you can start the above process of waiting for the dog to sit before having the leash put on.

Occasionally, we get a dog who is hand-shy with collars. Any time you go near his collar with your hand, he backs away or mouths your hand. In this case, you will need to do a little extra work. Put the leash away and sit down with the dog. Reach your hand out about halfway between you and the dog's collar, and reward the dog out of your other hand. Simply the view of a hand can be enough to create arousal, so you will need to look at body language to know where to start. You need to do several successful repetitions at each level, wherein the dog's ears and tail are relaxed, before you move to the next level. You will get to the point where you may touch the collar and treat. Then start gently massaging the neck on the underside before you reward. Initially, avoid working the top of the neck, as this seems to create the most resistance and potentially blocks the dog's vision. Once you are able to take the dog's collar from any point on the neck, you will need to be able to tug a bit on the collar, then spin the collar around to find the metal ring while the dog remains calm. Then you'll need to be able to approach the dog and take the collar. If you've been sitting and doing this exercise, you'll need to kneel, then perhaps sit in a chair, and then stand, and then take a few steps toward the dog. Taking this slowly is imperative because it is really easy to undo the work you've done on this skill. This process is called **counterconditioning**. The definition of this is changing the perception of something from

Once a dog learns that the leash means sit quietly and good things happen, the fun can begin!

negative to positive. The dog used to shy away from the hand near the collar, and now he thinks having his collar is cool because it results in great treats and praise and rubs. Keep in mind that this process can take days to months, and that time period is dictated by your dog, not by you.

Now let's go to the leg-lifting example as a first step toward being able to go outside on a leash. You are standing at the door with your dog on his leash. He is sitting and looking happily at you. At this moment, you may reward the behavior by opening the door and running with him to a favorite marking spot. Not all dogs do this, but for the ones who love to mark (and it's not all male dogs, either!), this is a wonderful example of a **life reward** or **natural reward**. It's cheap and easy, and won't put weight on your dog!!

OK, so now you either have a happy, non-marking dog at the door, or a happy, marking dog outside. What to do next? Either way, you need to proceed (hopefully with some grace!) to the next step. The next step is always to have your dog **focus** on you. If your dog is not paying attention to you, you don't have a dog. How does one accomplish this humongous task? It's very simple. You just wait! That's right, you simply wait for your dog to look at you. When he does, when he's looking right into the pupils of your eyes, you reward that. The clicker is so useful for this activity because some dogs are real "scanners." They are constantly looking around, checking everything out. They don't look at any one thing for very long. German shepherds, in particular, are big scanners. Generally speaking, the more anxious the dog, the more scanning he'll do.

No matter where your dog is, if he's on a leash, the unspoken law is that he needs to check in with you every few seconds. Of course, the best time to do this is the very first day you bring your puppy home, but at this point most of us have adults with issues, not puppies. The next best thing would be to have a dog of any age who only sees the leash when you are doing this activity with him. In other words, no walking on a leash during this time. For many owners, this is impossible, so you just need to be as consistent as possible.

Standing and waiting for your dog to look at you, you may wonder when it will all end! Patience. Standing inside and practicing this is likely to be much more effective than standing outside. Minimize the distractions (kids, cats, other dogs, doorbells, TV, radio, husbands, wives, etc) so that the dog has little reason to divert his attention from you. Do this for short bursts, several times per day. The more places in the house you can do this, the better off you are. If your dog is a ball (or stick or toy) fanatic, use the ball as a game-ending reward. Your dog will tell you when he's ready for the next step, by starting to happily and quickly look up at you. Now you need to start moving. Take one step. Take it backwards. Stop and wait for your dog to look at you. Once you've rewarded him, take another step, this time in any direction. The poorest choice for a direction would be forward, because most dogs quickly learn that if you're going that way, they are also going that way. But they move faster than we do, and they are very easily distracted, so we want to set our dogs up for being

Sharon has taught Jasmine leash etiquette; when the leash is attached, pay attention to "Mommy" and good things will happen.

successful. Do several mini-sessions a day of this moving around. A step here, two steps there. Your dog will start to shadow you. I call this activity, "The Dance." With consistent practice, your dog will move with you all through the house, and you should even be able to walk through an entire room for one reward!

Now let's go back to the door. You should be able to discern that you need to reward your dog for each little success, and build upon it. At the door, your dog is now sitting and waiting patiently for you

This dog is extremely excited to greet someone. Can you imagine how difficult this might be if she were reactive? Note that not one of her feet is on the floor!

to put on his leash. He then looks lovingly up at you, and you reward him for that. Your next step may be to turn and look at the door handle. Remembering that dogs are masters of body language and faster movers than humans, you want to reward your dog for staying put when you look at the door. Once he's done this several times, you will reward him for staying while you reach for the handle, and then touch the handle, and then jiggle the handle. Proceed through each miniscule step, if necessary, until you are standing at the door with your dog sitting, looking at you and the door is open. Don't forget that in order to consider each step a success, you'll need to be able to replicate this over several training sessions in several days. If your dog has a setback, simply go to the step before and rework that a bit before moving on.

It is impossible for me to overemphasize the importance of this activity. Even owners of non-reactive dogs tend to gloss over this critical skill and then complain when their dog pulls on the leash. If your dog is reactive, you simply cannot expect to progress in your training without putting time and effort into this foundation skill. So take the time now, while your dog is still "vacationing," do it, and practice, practice, practice.

Your first step outside is going to be a giant leap in your training regime. Your dog is on his leash, sitting and looking at you. The door is wide open, and you are about to take a step. One step. And then stop, and wait for your dog to sit and/or look at you. Your dog has just been placed on a new planet, for all he knows!! We may not think that it's very interesting outside, but the smells and sounds can be overwhelming to a dog. Patience. The longer the dog takes to look at you the first time, the more potent the reward should be! If this door leads out to a fenced-in yard, the first time your dog looks at you, click and drop the leash and run around and play! If he is not in a secure area, you can run and jump around and play with your dog, or go to his marking tree! Or, you can use a **long line**.

Long lines, in my opinion, are one of the best tools that we can use with dogs. You can purchase them at any pet food store, or sometimes even more inexpensively at a feed store that sells equestrian gear. You can even find nice tubular lines at sporting goods stores where mountain climbing gear is sold. They come in all lengths from 10 feet to 100 feet, and in all different materials, from cotton web to leather to nylon. I like to knot my long line every 5 to 10 feet so it doesn't slip through my hands so easily. You should either have a handle on one end or a large knot, with the clasp at the other to attach to your dog's collar. Make sure the clasp is strong enough that it won't break if your dog hits the end quickly and with some force. I like to use a 50-foot long line.

If you are going to use a long line for your outside focus activities, attach it AND your leash to the collar. Hold onto the leash for the activity, and have the long line on the ground. When you want to reward your dog by running around with him, drop the leash and pick up the long line, or simply be prepared to step on it if he seems to be moving quickly away from you. The long line is an excellent way to teach your dog that there is some freedom in being outside, but there are limits, and the really good stuff happens when he's near you.

If your dog gets excited and pulls on the leash or barks, simply do nothing. Just wait. This is, after all, training time. Any response

Acacia loves her long line because it means we are going to do something really fun, like practice herding sheep, or run and chase the ball in the park. In my right hand is her 6 foot leash for when other people are nearby and I need more control.

you may have to him at this moment is likely to either be ignored or construed as reinforcement for the current behavior. You will need to be watching carefully for signs of over-stimulation. While you may stand and wait a long time for a quiet dog to look at you, a dog who barks for 15 seconds straight should return to the house. Try again later. For this reason, it is best to start in the quietest area outside, during the quietest time of the day. The fewer kids and dogs and people in general the dog sees, the more quickly you are going to be successful.

Over time, you will be moving around more with your dog. It is not imperative for him to be looking at you while you are moving, but once you work up to 3 steps, then 4 and 5 and so on, your dog should check in with you every once in a while. This process of moving with a person on a leash, without pulling, is called loose leash walking. Your dog should be learning that hanging out with you is a Very Good Thing, and it's OK to look around and sniff, but he must check in with you every five or so seconds.

Mollie is focused and happy, walking with Kim. This is the result of consistent work.

Fencing. Fences can be a Godsend, and yet they can be a nightmare as well. There are obviously many different kinds of fences. Some of them are great solutions, and others leave much to be desired. The main purpose of fencing is to contain your dog and allow him to run around (preferably with you, as opposed to by himself), or eliminate or play with other dogs. In general, fencing should not take the place of walking your dog and taking him places regularly. Dogs need to be a part of our society in order to maintain appropriate generalization and social skills. Some of us have dogs that are so reactive that a fenced in yard is currently the only option. But this should be a short-term management strategy rather than a lifetime of banishment from the larger world. Leashes are safe, for sure, but they are also very limiting. Dogs need to run, and fencing allows this. But if this containment is not safe, its use is a failure.

Your best bet is a solid privacy fence. The construction doesn't matter (PVC and wood are the most common), but preventing dogs from looking out at other dogs or people from peering in is the vital component. A 6-foot fence is better than a 4-foot fence to minimize the chances your dog will scale the fence. Having said that, I've known many dogs who have escaped even higher fences. Digging under the fence is another issue that may need to be addressed, and it is possible to run some of the fencing underground in an effort to deter digging. It is also possible to install posts, boards, or wire six inches below the surface to achieve the same result.

We are dealing with the safe containment of a fearful or reactive dog in this book. Each dog is different in terms of the things that scare him or set him off, but visual stimuli are usually involved to some degree. This is why a privacy fence is so preferred over chain link, split rail with wire, or electric fencing. Let's look at each of these.

Chain link is relatively inexpensive to install. It can be covered in nice colors, such as green or black epoxy, and it usually safely contains a dog. But the dog can see out. Usually, the dog can see other dogs being walked down the road, or school children walking and skipping along, teasing each other, screaming and flailing. Sometimes that teasing becomes teasing the dog. They may throw sticks or stones at the dog, or they may run up to the dog, who is now barking, and then run away. All of that motion is stimulating to even a non-reactive dog. Then there are the cats and squirrels that frequent the area, not to mention skateboards, bikes and joggers. While a dog may be stimulated by the sounds or smells of such goings-on, the visual aspect is usually the final straw that sets him off.

It is possible to add slats to the chain link. These also come in different colors and may be made of metal or PVC. They usually are installed on a slanted angle to the ground, and can cut up to 90% of visibility. If you already have chain link, this addition is the best way to upgrade your fence and help your dog. Bamboo slats have also become popular. Split rail fencing can be very attractive, but it is difficult to create a visual barrier out of it.

Electric fencing is the poorest possible choice for fencing. Not only can the dog see out, and others see in, but also no one knows where the line is. Dogs and people may enter the property, not knowing where the line is. If your reactive dog has had lots of opportunities to bark at passersby, this may have built his frustration level to the point where he may nip, or worse. And if it's a stray dog, your dog is at risk for being cornered in a fight. Electric fences run on the principle that your dog does not want to experience the discomfort of a shock, so he'll be unwilling to cross that boundary, and may get cornered and injured in a dogfight. It also makes him more visible; many North American cities and towns have had rashes of dogs being stolen out of yards and sold for research. It is just that much easier to toss a poisoned treat onto a yard with electric fencing than it is to toss it over a six-foot fence. While it's not tremendously common, there have been a number of documented cases of the shock collars malfunctioning and emitting a continuous current, resulting in severe and potentially deadly burns on your dog's neck. If you have a dog with a high prey drive, he may be willing to take a hit when exiting the property to chase a cat, bunny or squirrel, but not so willing to take that hit to come back in. Now you have a reactive dog on the outside of your fence.

My writing hand was permanently damaged when I rescued a lost dog off a very busy two-lane highway. This Lab was standing in the middle of the road, about to be hit by a tractor-trailer. I managed to get a hold on her collar, but she spun around out of fear and twisted around twice, trapping two of my fingers in her collar. Why was this dog loose? Her electric fence collar batteries died and hadn't been replaced. This happens regularly. That dog was lucky. My fingers weren't.

Despite all of these reasons to avoid electric fencing, the most compelling reason involves the mechanisms it uses: positive punishment and negative reinforcement. There is so much fallout that comes with using this sort of fencing that I wonder that it is so popular. Certainly, there are many dogs who seem to adjust and never have a problem with this type of training and fencing. But there are also many dogs whose stress level increases with the use of electric fences. Sometimes that stress results in a bite. And sometimes that bite results in euthanasia. This can all be avoided by installing a solid fence.

There is a concept that goes along with all of these types of management that needs to be introduced here. It is called "barrier frustration." Think of an electric fence in use. The dog is outside, safely contained. The dog is already a bit anxious in general. School kids walk by on their way home, and tease the dog a little bit. They walk up on the curb, knowing the dog won't get them. The dog is frustrated now, because each time he gets close to the boundary, he hears that warning beep. Having learned that the beep might result in a shock on his neck (the link between which he is not capable of understanding), he stays back. But he wants to get to the kids, to sniff them, perhaps. Or to jump up on them or be petted. He ends up feeling frustrated. This happens daily, and it happens with others, too. Joggers run by, some of them jogging with their dogs. The dogs may bark at him, and then disappear. He may see the mailman or the delivery person come and go, as well. But he can't get to any of them.

This frustration builds over time, until eventually the socially eager dog becomes barky, and the bark sounds more and more "aggressive." One day, he reaches his final straw. A person whom he's seen day in and day out going by his fence line, comes up onto the property, or the battery dies. The dog is now free of his barrier. A dog who, at one time, may have simply run up to the person, now rushes at the person. Perhaps he just nips the person on the heel or the behind, or even the hand. If that's all he does, we're all lucky. But with each successive occasion, the aggressive display will worsen. Nips become bites and attacks.

How do we know which dog will be a good candidate for this type of fence and which dog will deteriorate? There are too many variables to know for sure. As in everything, genetics play a role, as do socialization, training, personality, environment, and opportunity to go places other than the yard. Suffice it to say, electric fences in particular, and fences that do not provide a visual barrier in general, are poor containment choices for any dog, and especially for a reactive dog.

Occasionally I am faced with a client who informs me that fencing is against regulations for the community in which they live. This is a very difficult situation all around. The dog is reactive, fearful, and possibly aggressive. It's often a larger dog, high energy, with high exercise requirements. The owners have installed electric fencing to allow the dog to go outside to run around and eliminate. They love their dog, but have no time to exercise the dog properly. They have just spent a fair amount of money to install this fencing, thinking it would resolve some issues, such as chewing out of boredom. Instead, it results in an aggressive dog. It's very difficult for me, as a trainer, to tell them that they should discontinue the use of the electric fencing, as it is increasing their dog's aggression, and to make time to walk or run with the dog twice per day, or re-home the dog. It's difficult to heartbreaking to deal with these issues. There is simply no simple solution.

I also, fairly frequently, get phone calls from concerned and irritated owners who are at their wits' end. The problem? The dog is barking aggressively at the door, and acting "in an aggressive manner when visitors come in." The dog has nipped, perhaps more than once, and has possibly even broken the skin. I rarely need to even ask the one question which I know will be answered in the affirmative...do you have electric fencing? It's almost inevitable. Yes.

Placement of a fence is an important consideration as well. Your best bet is to limit your fencing placement (regardless of the type of fencing used) to the part of your property with the least traffic. In most cases, this would be the backyard. For those folks who intend to keep their electric fencing, moving it to the backyard diminishes the barrier frustration and alleviates some of the trouble.

Tie-outs. If you do not have a fence at all, but you want to leave your dog outside to get a breath of fresh air, using a tie-out may be a reasonable option for you. You can find a wire cable, which has a clip at either end, at your pet food store. They, like the long lines, come in a variety of lengths. You can also find a metal spiral anchor that you screw into the ground, and attach the tie-out to it. You can also attach the clip to a solid fixture. I have one wrapped around my porch post, and clipped to itself. You can use a tree or a laundry line. These are great for camping, too! They are also available in a trolley format, wherein you attach the line between two trees, and there is a runner line on a wheel. Again, this is the sort of thing you don't want to be using in your front yard, particularly if you have a reactive dog. Keep your dog's tie-out limited to a part of your yard where there is little activity over which to react. Your best use of this tool is to be out there with your dog, doing training with him. Practice those recalls!

Car. What a strange concept. Using the car as crate. Yet I do it all the time. When my dogs are not sure what's going on, their spot of choice is always going to be the car. I travel lots with my dogs. They often accompany me to lessons or to the store. We take the car to go to hiking spots twice per day. The car is a wonderful place. It's one more type of safe containment that I can use in addition to the

Montana looks for reasons to bark in the car. Her bark is loud and startling to the driver, which can be dangerous. Repeated barking becomes self-reinforcing and should be managed by crating.

ones mentioned above. Of course, your dog must find the car to be a wonderful source of good things. If he doesn't, we have some work to do! You can use free-shaping to achieve similar results to what you did with the crate. You can feed your dog his dinner in the car for a few days or weeks, until he decides it's a great place to be. If your dog feels ill in the car, abstain from feeding him for several hours before you take him for a ride. Ginger snaps may help settle his tummy. Signs that he doesn't feel well in the car include foaming, vomiting and diarrhea. Whining, crying, pacing, barking and scratching are more likely to be anxiety-based than car sickness.

Ruff lays calmly in his crate. When the hatch is closed, he is completely covered and can't see out the windows. It also provides him with a safety measure in the case of a short stop or accident.

The best advice I can give is to crate your dog in the car. This can be difficult for folks with small cars and large dogs. But if you are truly dedicated to helping your pooch be able to learn that the world is not a scary place, you will try your best to find a way to crate him in your car. The crate should be covered. Yes, that's right; your dog will be in a crate, safely contained within the vehicle and completely covered so that he does not see things that stimulate him. You may need to do this for months. Dogs tend to bark at people on the street, people they see driving vehicles sitting next to them at traffic lights, dogs walking down the street, birds, and the list goes on. My older dog has a fixation with water towers and those balls on high-tension wires, and her barking is quite obsessive in these cases. She barks at little else. My Belgian sheepdog barks only at other dogs while she is in the car.

While you are crating and covering your dog in the car, you are teaching him to be quiet while riding. You are also helping to diminish those glucocorticoids. But we can enhance the process if we can classically condition the concept of being quiet in the car by feeding treats while riding in the car. This can be difficult to impossible to downright dangerous for some circumstances, and you may need to move the crate around or lift part of the cover to access the crate, or even have someone ride with you at first. This activity is so important, however, that I have had some students make next to no progress with their dogs for weeks and months until they finally broke down and tried the covered crate in the car. At that point, the dogs' ability to learn skyrocketed.

If crating is impossible, you can use a Calming Cap on your dog. This is a light cloth face mask which covers the eyes, much like a horse mosquito mask or a falconry hood. They are available at Premier.com.

The most critical aspect of management for you to remember is this: How can I contain my dog safely so that he doesn't get into trouble or get injured, while meeting all of his needs AND not permitting him to practice unwanted behaviors (barking, lunging, growling) or be over-stimulated or overwhelmed?

In order to begin to work with our dear companion who finds the world a scary and frustrating place, we need to keep him calm and quiet for at least a week. Remember those glucocorticoids? We need their level to diminish in our dog's body. The longer they've been coursing around, the longer you will likely need to keep your dog calm and quiet. This is no easy feat. For some owners, it means no walks. For others, it may mean waking up at 5 a.m., before dawn, to minimize the risk of running into other people and/or dogs on their morning jaunt. It may require that you have no visitors to your home for a week or two. It probably means no trips to the vet (unless it's an emergency) or to the pet food store. We want the dog to be calm and relaxed. Playing ball in the yard is a good exercise option. In the meantime, you'll be starting to teach some new skills, so you'll be occupying his brain, at least. Use lots of crate time, and experiment with calming touch. Give him jobs to do: stuff his Kong® with his food, or fill those roller-balls with food and let him push that around to get the food out. Broadcast some of his meals in the back yard so he has to hunt for it rather than just eat it out of a bowl. (You may have to teach him about this at first by tossing just a few pieces and helping him to find them.) This activity uses his body, his brain *and* his nose, which is one canine sense we don't use enough in our training! Hunting for food keeps his head down, too, which encourages calm behavior, rather than the stimulation of scanning. Give him a good raw meaty bone to chew, or a rawhide. Do lots of free-shaping with him to keep him busy, teach him new tricks, and stimulate his creative juices!

While you're keeping your dog calm, you and he will be learning new training skills.

THE REAL STUFF

Welcome to the beginning of your new dog!

Presumably, you've been busy during the past week or so, reading this book's suggestions, finding a better food for your dog, learning how to free-shape and use calming touch. You've been keeping your dog calm but "getting his yahoos out" by throwing a stick, ball or toy for him. You've been walking him in places and during times where he is unlikely to be stimulated by the things that set him off. If you've been doing this, you may start to see a dog whose eyes look less like dinner plates. He may bark less often, less intensely, or stop barking more quickly. He may even experience better sleep. His stools might become firmer. All sorts of neat things start to happen when those horrid stress hormones dissipate. It's different for every dog.

You have also been making a list of the things that set your dog off. Does he bark at dogs while he's in the car? Does he growl at people who come to the door? Does he bark at children but not at adults? Does he seem to be fine with other dogs until he's sniffed them for a few seconds? Is he fine with puppies but not adult dogs? Or is it the other way around? Is he tolerant of people walking down the street but not someone who suddenly appears from around the corner? List all of the triggers that you can remember. For how long have they been going on, and when did they start? Describe the behaviors in as precise detail as possible. Also, try to recall your typical response to these behaviors. It is wise, at this point, to start keeping a journal so that you may refer to it in the future. Progress can be slow, so seeing it on paper can help to keep you motivated.

When I realized that my Belgian Sheepdog was having reactive issues with other dogs, it was difficult to find a pattern at first. While I didn't know it early on, she was always a sensitive, reactive dog. Her troubles really started after I spayed her at age two years (she was a show dog prior to that). After a while, I noticed that she had the most difficulty with Labrador Retrievers, particularly black ones. As soon as she saw one, her tail would go up in a large, still arc. She became very still. Her ears were erect and facing the dog. Initially, she would approach or allow the other dog to approach, and her tail would wag slowly. Within seconds she would be in a confrontation with the other dog. There was always lots of noise and open-mouth flailing, but she would often end up biting the other dog in the face, usually near the eye or on the nose. No major harm was ever done, just usually a small contusion on the other dog. But it was horribly embarrassing for me, obviously too stimulating for her, scary for the other dog and for the other owner, and it was inappropriate behavior.

While I was trying to figure out this pattern, I am sure she was giving me body language to tell me that she was uncomfortable with certain situations. Unfortunately, I was unskilled at reading her signs, and the result was that she learned that she couldn't fall back on me to protect her or take control of the situation, so she began preemptive strikes on other dogs. Her survival tactic was to get to the other dog before it got to her. If she saw a dog from even a great distance (75 yards) and she was off leash, she would run straight for the other dog and initiate a scuffle. As I watched these dramas unfold over time, I realized that it didn't much matter what the other dog's body language said. She had learned a pattern of behavior that worked for her. More often than not, it appeared to me that the other dog was friendly. Eventually I noticed that it seemed to be Labs that set her off, and later still I realized that it was probably any dog that she felt might try to jump on her. Labs tend to be exuberantly social dogs, and play with other dogs far longer into their lives than most other breeds. This exuberance in play was obviously something that frightened my Belgian, and she felt powerless to control it.

In retrospect, many of these dogs were probably equally poor at reading other dogs' body language. In my particular region of the states, many dogs are poorly socialized. They simply are not given many opportunities to play, off leash, with other dogs. Whether this had meaningful impact on my dog's particular situation is simply a matter of speculation. However, it is rather common for some dogs, adolescents in particular, and often Labs, Lab mixes, Boxers and Boxer mixes, to play hard or attempt to play with any dog that comes along. They run right up, expecting the other dog to be equally willing to play. Attempts to decline play are seemingly ignored and the scuffle can be the result, particularly when neither dog is being managed well by its owner.

Once I realized what was going on, my immediate treatment for this behavioral issue was to keep her on leash, at all costs. This severely cramped my style, as we like to hike miles through the woods and in parks. But I simply could not risk this liability; Acacia was reactive to bike riders, joggers, and other people in general, as well. We will address these other triggers later, but for now I will use the reactivity to dogs in our initial discussion. So, on the leash she went, twice a day for our walks. I knew that hollering at her or physically punishing her in response to these behaviors was not a viable option, and yet I wasn't sure how to proceed. But I did know that positive reinforcement has wonderful results in obedience training, so I started there.

STUFF-A-DOG

The best place to start when training any dog, at any age, is with Stuff-a-Dog [7]. Also dubbed, "stuff-the-puppy" by some of my students, this is classical conditioning at its best. This activity teaches your dog a positive association between a sound and something good, in this case, food. It teaches name recognition, focus, and recall. Here's how to do it:

Place a yummy treat in your dog's mouth. While he's chewing, say his name one time.

Place another yummy treat in your dog's mouth. While he's chewing it, say his name one time.

Repeat this process, varying your intonation in saying his name. You may include a nickname that you use for your dog, too. Sometimes say his name like you're happy, sometimes sad, sometimes angry, or frustrated, loud, quiet, silly, and so on.

You can do Stuff-a-Dog in several different ways. You can use a handful of his food before dinner time. You can do Stuff-a-Dog for 30 seconds. You can take a biscuit and break it up in small pieces and do Stuff-a-Dog until the biscuit is gone. However you do it, you want to do about 5000 Stuff-a-Dogs over a several (usually 6-8) week period.

This is not a conscious thought process on the part of your dog. This is associative learning. We want your dog to have a very positive reaction toward you when he hears his name. Remembering that dogs do not generalize well, you will want to do this activity (and any training) in every room of the house in which your dog is permitted, facing every direction, and with your body in different postures (standing, sitting, kneeling on the floor, sitting on the floor, and lying down).

While you are building the power of your dog's name, it will be in your best interest to avoid saying your dog's name in his presence unless you are speaking to him. If you are talking about the dog, say, "the dog," or "the fluffy beast," or "the toothy one." But don't say to the other person in the room, "Guess what Fluffy did today? Blah blah blah. Can you believe that Fluffy?" First of all, you are undoing all of your hard work on Stuff-a-Dog! Second of all, it is really difficult for our dogs to tease out the meaningful verbiage from the (to the dog) unintelligible stuff. Make it simple. If you are talking TO your dog, say his name. If you are talking ABOUT your dog, use a code name. Or just say, "the dog." If you do mistakenly say your dog's name in conversation and he looks at you, for doG's sake, smile and praise him!

Occasionally, we have already used up whatever good association there will ever be with a name. Each time Acacia had another confrontation, I would scream her name in a feeble attempt to stop her. Aside from the fact that she either didn't hear me calling her or interpreted my calling her as a vote of support for her behavior, she began to associate that sound ("Acacia") with heightened arousal and emotion. Her very name became a negative stimulus to her. There have also been theories that suggest that the sounds "s," "sh," and "ch" in a name mimic alert sounds in many species. The name "Acacia" (pronounced, "ah-kay-sha") has one of those sounds. Wishing to make as good a start as possible, I began to change her name using Stuff-a-Dog. As it turns out, she responded to me a few times when I said the word, "puppy," so that's what I started calling her! This name had the added benefit of people occasionally happening to say her name to her ("Aw, what a pretty puppy!")

If you feel that you have created a negative association with your dog's name, consider changing it. It doesn't have to be a permanent change; I used, "Puppy" for about a year, and once I started to get really nice, calm behaviors from her, I went back to using, "Acacia."

She now responds nicely to it. If you do decide to use a different name for your dog, try to use soft sounds rather than sharp, staccato sounds. You might also consider using a word that evokes real happiness. Try to say, "Happy" and feel grumpy or angry!! It doesn't work, does it? Part of changing your dog's name involves a start on your part to feel positive emotion for a dog who may have had you frustrated, angry, embarrassed, and/or upset for a long time. It's time to change that habit and to get out of that rut.

The goal of Stuff-a-Dog is not just for you to get your dog's attention, but also to classically condition your dog to come to you when he hears his name. You really want this response to be like a knee-jerk response. However, in order to achieve this goal, you need to start doing your Stuff-a-Dog in the house, and then do it in the car, on your walks, and everywhere you go. Do just a little bit here and there, until it's really pervasive in your dog's life. Once you've reached your 5000-repetition criterion, you can do fewer repetitions, but you do still want to always do some.

YOU'LL HAVE 'EM EATING FROM YOUR HAND

There is no rule which states that a domesticated dog must eat from a bowl. It's funny how we become so embroiled in our own expectations of life.

The suggestion that I feed my dog out of my hand and not out of a food bowl was met with much resistance. Once I had time to think about it, I agreed to do so, and I ended up doing just that, twice a day, for nearly a year. The manner in which I did this varied. Sometimes I did a bunch of Stuff-a-Dog, using several pieces of kibble at a time, and sometimes I hand-fed her while I was doing other training. Once in a while I was in too much of a rush and I fed her out of her bowl, or part of her meal out of a bowl, or even off the floor. A few times I broadcast her food in the backyard and let her forage for it. It gave her something to do and helped her burn off some extra energy. Whatever you decide to do, try to be as open-minded as possible when it comes to training activities for your reactive dog.

The reason for hand feeding is that you want your dog to learn that all good things come from you. Every treat, every meal, access to outside and to the car, access to toys and walks, petting and scratching come from you. All good things come from you. This is another classically conditioned activity and concept for your dog. It is very much a process and the understanding will not take place quickly.

PIRANHA DOG

What if your dog has a "hard mouth"? What if, every time you offer him food, he snatches it from your hand, leaving you to bleed to death? How do you deal with that nasty behavior?

Actually, this is a very good barometer of the emotional state of your dog. A dog with a hard mouth is likely in a state of high arousal. The reason for this state of arousal can vary from dog to dog and from day to day within a dog. Is he very hungry? Is he afraid of being teased? Is there another dog nearby who might compete with him for that food? Perhaps the food being offered is really delicious and he can't wait to get more. Is he hearing loud or scary noises while he's attempting to eat?

This activity can be functional in more ways than one. If your dog has a hard mouth all of the time, you will need to teach him how to have a softer mouth. This is a dog who is rarely calm. He is in a perpetual state of hype. The best way to change this is to feed him a piece of food out of the palm of your hand, with your hand below his chin. If your hand is placed correctly, he will have to tuck his chin toward his chest to get the food. Sometimes a dog will just stand up (if he's sitting) and back up, or just back up (if he's standing) so that he can maintain a strong bite. If this happens, just close your hand and/ or remove your hand so that he can't grab at the food. He will need to learn that the only way he gets food is to have a soft mouth. In order to have a soft mouth, he must relax his jaw. If his head is tucked, the jaw must be soft. If you have a dog who backs up to maintain a strong bite, start asking for a sit or waiting for a sit before you even offer the food. This is likely to take many repetitions, but it's well worth the wait. Gentle, calm praise can help to soothe the beast.

If your dog's mouth is only hard sometimes, then it is a very good indicator that something in his environment is creating arousal. If this is the case, then you have a very good cue to move your dog to a safer, less threatening place. This is not a cue to be ignored; in fact, this is one sign that should never be ignored. It is one sign to me and to my students that a dog is having trouble. A hard mouth may also indicate that something is taking place internally. You are less likely to figure this out, at least for a while. It could be anything from allergies to a toothache. This sort of issue is likely to start up quickly, and in a dog whose mouth is not usually hard.

Precious learned to take treats nicely from her owner, who feeds her from underneath. This forces her jaw to relax and her bite to be soft.

Once your dog begins to relax his mouth, you can, and should, start to offer the food out of your fingertips as opposed to the palm of your hand. This requires a more precise and delicate effort on the part of your pooch, and therefore, more thought. This is, after all, an operant activity.

Another method for hand-feeding a dog with a hard mouth is to place a piece of food in the dog's mouth from the side, and put it far back in his mouth so that he has to relax and open it to get the treat. You still want his head to be lowered a bit, as opposed to raised up with nose pointing skyward. You will, of course, decide whether you feel comfortable doing this activity with your dog, and you are not likely to have others do this with your dog. This can be a difficult behavior to do because it's awkward. It takes much practice, but once you have the hang of it, and your dog starts to understand the new routine, it becomes easier. I found this to be a very difficult activity with my dog, but I've used it successfully with other dogs.

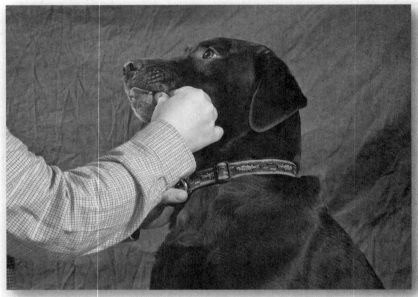

An alternative, and usually more difficult method of treating a dog with a hard mouth is to feed him from the side. This comes as a surprise to most dogs at first; eventually, they learn to just "suck" the treat in.

REACH OUT AND TOUCH SOMEONE

Earlier, we discussed the concept of finger targeting or hand targeting. This is the second training activity I prescribe for owners of reactive dogs. I have them spend about a week working on just point-and-click, then they attach the word, "here" (for finger targeting) or "touch" (for hand targeting) simultaneous to the nose touch for about a week, and then they can finally begin to use the word as a cue. Their dog's knowledge of this skill is still tenuous at best at this point, and it is important for them to practice moving around a room, stopping every so often and holding out a finger or hand for the dog to find and touch when he hears the cue. Once the dog is truly enjoying this activity, they begin to move from room to room, calling the dog with, "Fluffy, here!" and having the dog find and touch a finger or hand. At this point, they move to the quieter parts of outside: porch, garage, deck or driveway, at times when there is little activity.

The more distracting an environment, the more exciting the praise and reward must be. When inside, with no one around, your dog might work for that Brussels sprout. But the moment you open the door to the outside world, you had better have a hungry dog and that filet mignon ready, and lots of it! Or perhaps your dog finds a tennis ball even better. It is your responsibility to have those things for your dog in order to really drive home the notion that you ARE the best thing in the world.

Start Climbing the Rungs

Set up a program for yourself and your dog. Science tells us that an 80% success rate is optimal for learning. Anything higher is likely to lead to boredom. Anything lower indicates that the skill has not been sufficiently learned. Use this as a criterion for everything you do with your dog.

Once your dog responds to your finger by touching it with his nose 80% of the time, or eight out of ten times per session for eight out of ten sessions (or four out of five sessions), you may move on to the next step. In this case, it's labeling the behavior with the word, "here." Of course, this particular activity is classical conditioning, so there are no operant criteria to reach, just many associations. The next criterion is for your dog to respond to the cue 80% of the time in four out of five training sessions, in that particular context. What is the context? Are you working in the living room, or every room of the house? Are you working when there's no one else present, or is the entire family there? Select one variable and change it, or add to it. If you've only been working in one area of the house, add other areas to the routine. Then add people (family members to start). Then add other pets, perhaps. Or add music or the TV.

In my classes for reactive dogs, we always say, "Boring is Good." You always want to have a calm and quiet dog at one level before moving on to the next level. You want your dog to have an appearance that says, "nothin' doing" before you move on. We often want to push our dogs to do more before they are ready, and when we do, we regret it. Stick with the mantra, "Boring is Good." It'll help!

Once you go outside, try to work when there is little going on out there. Just being outside with all of those smells we can't smell and sounds we can't hear can easily overwhelm your dog. Have patience and work toward that 80% rate of success. If your dog is having a difficult time reaching that goal, consider what's going on around him. Remember to give him plenty of time to figure things out. That might be 10 seconds or 30 seconds, as long as he seems to be on task. If he is looking at your or at your finger or hand but not touching it, just wait. If at any point he appears to be too distracted (looking around, barking, air sniffing for more than a few seconds), stop what you are doing and take your dog to the place you last worked him successfully. While you are moving him, encourage him to come with you but don't engage in any other form of interaction.

When he is able to do his point and click in a quiet part of his outside world, start increasing the distraction level. The options are endless as to how you can add distractions. They are often going to be unpredictable, and you will need to keep in mind that distractions can take the form of sound, sight, smell, vibrations, pheromones, and other stimuli that may be imperceptible to us. The more distracting the stimulus, the more intense and approving your response is going to be to his ability to focus on you and your finger or hand. Keep these sessions short, as few as two repetitions if the stimulus is very high. I have done as few as one repetition for my dog when I felt that it was nothing short of miraculous that she responded appropriately.

Remember that you want to get your 80% criteria in 80% of trials. This means that you will be best off doing each level over several days. While you want each step to be of similar stimulus rate, it doesn't necessarily mean that you must stand in exactly the same place each time. It is easy to write about this activity as a science, but the reality is that it is an art. It is an art because we don't live in an experimental laboratory. Events happen which we can't predict. You will get a feel for what your dog can and can't handle. Like everything else, the more of this you do, the more you'll be able to predict your dog's behavior. It really does help to keep a journal of these training events.

HOW'S TRICKS?

We tend to believe that behaviors such as sit, down, stand, come, and leave it are obedience skills, while behaviors such as spin, bow, speak, shake and roll over are tricks. The reality is, they're the same! I try to approach everything I teach a dog as a trick. They are, after all,

Clockwise from top left: Opie does "Budda"; Emett thinks he can do it better; Jaxon shakes a paw; Gabe does a majestic bow.

just things we ask them to do for which they may earn a reward, right? So let's act as if we are teaching our dogs a bunch of great tricks. It's a much more positive and fun attitude than teaching "obedience skills."

Your goal should be to teach your dog as many tricks as possible, whether you use free-shaping or lure-and-reward styles of training. The list of behaviors you can teach is endless, but at this point you are best advised to teach behaviors that you can easily get outside. Rolling over might be a great party trick, but it may not go over so well with your dog if it's raining or muddy. Asking him to do something that he's hesitant to do when there is something else "out there" that might be scary (i.e., laying down) is not a good tactic. He's already likely to be anxious, so asking him to do a trick that he doesn't know well yet, or one that requires a bit of discomfort, or that puts him in a position of disadvantage, will be a poor choice. Right now, work on behaviors such as sit, paw, bow, high-five, wave, a touch which requires the dog to jump up on his back legs to touch his nose to the palm of your hand, spin both ways, weave between your legs, back up, and come (on leash). These are just some examples; be creative. I will not be going into how to teach these behaviors, and I assume that your dog already has at least a few of these (sit and shake-a-paw are fairly basic tricks which many dogs learn early on in their careers).

Eventually, you will have a repertoire of tricks with your dog, and you can pick and choose those tricks and be variable in their use so as not to be boring, repetitive and predictable.

GOING FOR A RIDE IN THE CAR

Once you are able to keep your dog's focus on you in the house and all around your property, and your week or two of calm and quiet have passed, it is time to hit the road. Armed with the knowledge of the stimuli that trigger your dog as well as the list of tricks your dog knows well, you need to start going places and expanding your experience in the world as a team.

Earlier, I mentioned my Belgian sheepdog's reactivity to other dogs. Her case provides me with an illustration of how to proceed at this point in our trek.

I did not want to walk her around my neighborhood because ours is a neighborhood fraught with dogs. There are always dogs walking on leash, there are dogs barking inside their houses, dogs behind privacy fences, and dogs contained by electric fences. There are even dogs who traverse the neighborhood off leash. Sometimes we see a dog running with its owner or trotting along next to a bike. There was simply too much risk in walking her there, so I chose to drive her to parks and other places where we might see dogs at a distance.

Before I could walk her in the park I needed to know that she was paying attention to me, and I needed to remind her that she needed to pay attention to me in order to have the privilege of walking in the park. I needed to be able to have her in the car, open the car door for her and tell her "wait." You can teach this one of several ways, but perhaps the easiest way is to start at home. Open the door a bit and you will likely see your dog's head move forward. Shove a treat in her mouth, applying pressure toward the back of her head so her head remains in a neutral position, while saying, "wait." Practice this in your garage, if you have one, or with your dog on a leash held by someone in the car or attached to something unmovable, before doing

Sonora knows the hand signal for "wait." She has learned to stay put until Patrice asks her for the next move.

this in a less safe environment. In this manner, she learns her place when she hears, "wait."

When the car door was open and she was waiting patiently for me, I'd tell Acacia, "let's go" or "OK." This was her cue to jump out of the car. While her front paws were in the air, I'd say her name one time, making sure it was loud enough for her to hear, and happy enough a tone for her to be interested. The moment she looked at me, I'd click and treat, and then have her get back into the car. Once there, I'd "have a party." Having a party means that you reward your dog for a minimum of 20 seconds with all sorts of reinforcers.

Then I'd close the door for a few seconds and repeat the process. If she did well the second time, I'd do a few finger targets. It is imperative that these sessions are very short and very fun in the beginning.

If she did not orient toward me upon hearing her name within a certain period of time, she would unceremoniously be directed back into the car, the door would close, and I'd walk away for a short while. This could be anywhere from ten seconds to ten minutes, depending on the circumstances. If she was barking or whining in the car, I'd wait for calm and quiet behavior for a minimum of five seconds before I went back to the car.

You'll notice that the previous paragraph included three time periods: the amount of time it took her to look at me, the amount of time I let her be in the car, and the amount of time she needed to be quiet before I went back to the car. The amounts of time necessary for each dog are going to vary. For the first one, the amount of time needed to look at the person, I've worked with some dogs who needed 15 seconds to look at his person, while others seem to do fine with five seconds right off the bat. You will need to experiment with this one, but I suggest you start with ten seconds. These numbers are not based on scientific evidence but rather personal experience with many dogs over the years. Once your dog is able to handle looking at you within ten seconds 80% of the time over four or five sessions, begin to diminish the period of time until you reach about three seconds. The critical aspect to this exercise is that your dog learns that the expected behavior when coming out of the car is to look at you. In this manner, there is a limited opportunity for your dog to look around and find things that are scary. It seems as if some of our reactive dogs are anxious enough to look around and find things to which to react.

Kim tells Demon to wait (top photo). When she invites him out, she calls his name and waits for him to look at her, giving him ten seconds to do so (middle photo.) Demon checks in with Kim, earning a click and a treat (bottom photo).

There is a compulsive component to such behavior; these dogs have learned that there **are** scary things, and it is best to find them and bark at them to make them go away, and that the barking reduces anxiety. By working on structured focus, we are giving our dogs the chance to check out their world and check in to a source of calm.

The second measure, that of the period of time you leave your dog in the car, depends on the environment. If you are practicing this in the quiet of your garage, you may need less time in between than if you are in a park. If your dog is barking or is fixated on something, you will do well to keep your dog in a covered crate in the car. Typically, the higher the dog's arousal level, the longer it will take the dog to be calm before bringing him out again. If your dog is not barking but is generally not paying attention to you, you may need to leave him in the car for a shorter period of time than if he is making lots of noise.

The third measure is progressive and commensurate with your dog's skill level. Effective reinforcement takes place within about a half-second of the occurrence of the behavior, so three seconds of quiet is six times the duration of the maximum effective delay for reinforcement. Begin by waiting for three seconds of calm, and after an 80% success rate in that particular environment, increase the time to 5 seconds, then 7 or 8, then 10, 15 and 20 seconds of calm and quiet before bringing your dog out of the car again. Not only does this teach him that being quiet brings him the privilege of being out and with you, but also it reinforces the act of being calm. These dogs need to learn what calm feels like. So far, we've taught them to be calm and quiet in the house, but now, suddenly, there is a context shift. Since dogs don't generalize well, we need to teach "calm" in the car.

When you have your dog out of the car, and are asking him to respond to you, you will need to remember to wait for him to direct his attention to you. Experimentation will allow you to learn your dog's tendencies. Some dogs may require 12 seconds to look back at their person, during which time they are looking around but not making noise or quivering. Over time, that duration diminishes with practice. Other dogs have a very tiny window in which they are able to respond. Giving this dog 12 seconds to look back at you is almost certainly going to result in over-arousal. This dog may only have perhaps eight seconds in which to check in with you. If you have a difficult time getting your dog's attention on you, consider whether this is too distracting an environment. You may need to go back to an easier locale and get a quicker response time before moving up to this level of distraction.

It is imperative that you stay quiet while waiting for your dog to respond to your cue. The seconds may feel like an eternity as they tick away, but this is critical learning time for your dog. Talking to him may teach him to ignore you or to pay more attention to whatever it is that he **is** looking at, while repeating the cue may either confuse him or teach him to ignore your voice. The best way to teach a dog a skill is to label and reward a behavior. Remember; talking to a species whose forte is body language has its limits. You will be far more successful by waiting for desired behavior while providing limitations in time and management in the use of the car.

My goal for my dog was to be able to get her attention on me within three seconds of coming out of the car in a particular setting before moving to a more difficult setting. Even within one setting, there could be many variables skewing the results. There might be a person 50 yards away one time and no one within sight another time. This is why you are best advised to get an 80% success rate over several different days before moving on to the next level. While training in different situations may appear to be providing you and your dog with a structured setting, we can't possibly control everything that goes on around us.

As soon as I moved to the next higher level, I gave my dog up to ten seconds to respond to me when she got out of the car. With her, it was almost a guarantee that if I had to put her back in the car, she'd focus on me immediately the next time around. But this isn't the case with all dogs. I've done this with some dogs for weeks of class before they came around and seemed to internalize the expectation.

Either before you start this process, or as you are doing it, you should keep some sort of journal so that you can notate your progress. It really is better for you to make a list ahead of time of places in which you are going to train. Then list the criteria that you expect to achieve in each place. While this may appear to be overly scientific (and somewhat anal and annoying), it actually puts you in that place of a "benevolent leader." It allows you to know exactly what you are going to do, and removes much of the uncertainty in training a reactive dog. In short, it increases the chances of decreasing training time and trainer errors.

My list of training places might look like this:

Living room, dining room, kitchen, basement
Bedrooms, bathrooms, laundry room
Porch
Back yard
Front yard
Car in garage
Car in driveway
Car at nearby park, mid-morning
Car in remote area of grocery store parking lot
Car at nearby park, late afternoon

Each of these lines denotes a level of arousal more intense than the line before it. In order for me to move on to the next line, I need to be able to get and *keep* my dog's attention on me. At the first two levels, I am simply working my dog inside, with few distractions. At levels three, four and five, I can use the inside of the house like I would the car; if my dog does not pay attention to me within ten seconds, back in the house he goes. Once I start working my dog in the car, my training expectations look like the following:

Quiet in car at the start
Bring dog out of car for one target
Bring dog out of car; dog successfully responds to 3-5 cues
Bring dog out of car; dog successfully responds to 5-10 cues
Bring dog out of car; move around within about 10 feet of the car, dog responds successfully to about 5 cues
Bring dog out of car; move around within about 25 feet of the car, dog responds successfully to about 10-15 cues

You can see that in each place (list one), you will be working with your dog to achieve a series of goals (list two). But it's even more complicated than that; you want to get an 80% success rate at each of those levels! That means four out of five times (see charts) that you do each line, your dog must be successful (respond to you without

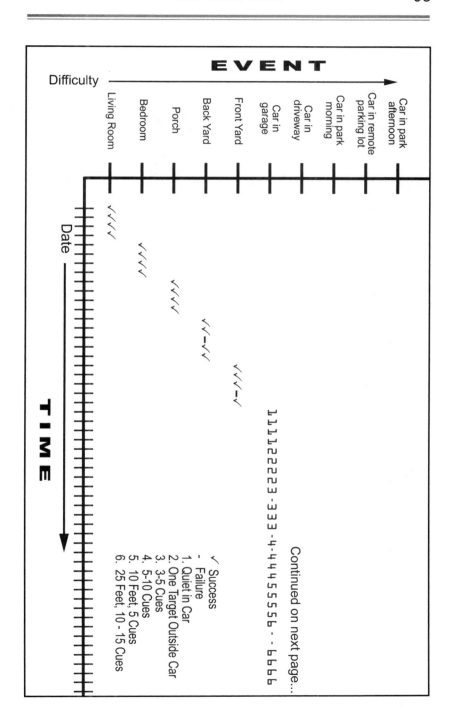

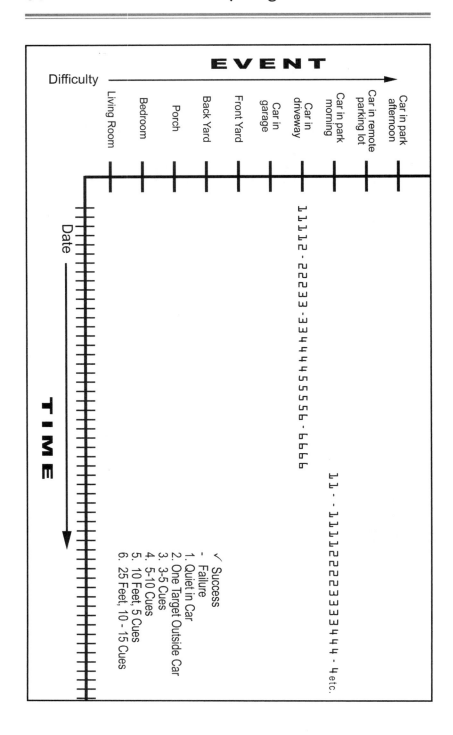

barking or fixating on other things). And THAT'S not even enough; if you really want to be sure that your dog is handling his new learning as well as possible, you should be doing each line on several different days.

Now you are attempting a very complicated web of training. It may seem to be an overwhelming proposition, but it truly is fairly simple if only you write it down. You can write it all down as if you are writing a diary, and jot down your work and successes on each date. However, I find note keeping much simpler if I can look at it all at once. Make yourself a chart, and make a simple code for yourself so that you can write down what you have accomplished in each training session. Use a check mark for successes and a dash for lack thereof You'll notice that I didn't use the word, "failure" here; I detest using that word in a learning situation because of the negativity it transmits in such circumstances.

By the time you have completed this part of your training, weeks or months may have gone by. But you will have a dog who is able to go quietly somewhere in a car in a covered crate, come out of the crate, get out of the car, pay attention to you, accept that there are other stimuli in the environment but not be bothered by them to the point where he must react to them, and enjoy tons of praise and loving and play and treats from you, his benevolent leader. WHEW! What a difference! You will be able to bring your dog out of the car, and while he may take the time to look around and see what is going on around him, he's calm enough to check back in with you, to look at you and do the things you ask him to do. Even if he finds something that is nerve-wracking, he is much more likely to be able to disengage from looking at it and return his gaze to you.

OUT FOR A DOG WALK

Using your car as a training tool allows you to use a framework for teaching your dog how to be calm while out in the Great Big Scary World. Using a car provides the potential for making training easy because it's a traveling crate. The downside to this is that we won't always have a car available to stick the dog into, should he respond poorly to a stimulus in his environment. This means that we need to teach our dogs to work with us for a longer duration and in a more variable situation than the one we have created near the car.

Going back to the training situation with Acacia, let's imagine that I've driven her to the parking lot of a large park. She's quiet, and I get her out of the car. She responds immediately to me when I say her name, and does several quick and happy finger targets upon request. I ask her for a sit, then a spin, a sit again, and a handshake. She's doing great, so I decide that it's time to move away from the car. I really want to walk her to give her exercise! So off we go, working on our focus and loose leash walking. I decide to hit a less-used trail in this particular park in order to avoid as much traffic as possible. We walk along a path in a wide-open field, and I can see another person walking his dog about 75 yards away. They are coming toward us.

The moment I realize that our paths are going to cross, I get a sinking feeling in my stomach. I feel my ears go back. I resist the temptation for my eyes to roll back in my head. I want to turn and run back to the car. I call this, "the 'oh shit' moment." It's that very moment when I just know what's going to happen because it happens every other time I find myself in this predicament. It just so happens that we are approaching the moment of truth.

Your dog senses this change in you. He may or may not see the other person and dog team. But the body language you are communicating and the pheromones you are producing, not to mention the tension on your leash, give a very clear message: something's wrong. If his leader is worried, your dog better be worried. You are a team, so you work together. In taking on the dreaded approach to this situation, you are telling your dog that you are not truly benevolent leader; therefore, he better be ready to step in.

This is the opportunity for you to make a change. As soon as you see the person and dog, put on your acting face. Act very happy that you see them, and take your dog off the path. Walk a 90-degree angle off the path, and keep walking and talking and praising your dog for coming with you and treating your dog all the way. You will need to find a critical threshold distance for your dog, after which point you can stop and ask your dog to sit. Praise and treat your dog, or play with a coveted toy, as the dog goes by. You may return to the path anywhere from a few seconds to a minute after the dog passes, and continue along your way.

In this series of photos, you can see that I see a person and dog approaching and move Acacia off the path so that she can pay attention to me and get good things from me as the dog passes. She has learned, through repetition, that a dog in the vicinity means treats. What a good thing!

In doing this task, you are accomplishing two goals. One, you are classically conditioning your dog (dog = good stuff). You also happen to be counterconditioning your dog's response to dogs. The subject (dog) used to elicit negative emotions within your dog. Over many repetitions of this, your dog will start to perceive the subject as something that indicates that good things are coming to him. In addition, it can be said that if you spend a reasonable period of time standing there, treating your dog as another dog passes, you are desensitizing your dog to the presence of other dogs. He is spending time being near (but not too close) other dogs, and nothing bad is happening. As a matter of fact, good things are happening. The second goal that you are accomplishing is that you are taking on that benevolent leadership. You are teaching your dog that you are taking care of him. Nothing bad is going to happen to him. You are not going to allow that bad dog to scare him or to get too close to him. As you can imagine, this must happen many times in order for him to internalize this, but every time you find yourself in this situation, you are strengthening this emerging belief.

If your dog begins to react poorly as you walk away from the other dog, keep walking. Continue to act as if you are truly happy about doing this, and keep going until your dog discontinues his effort to look at the other dog. As soon as he disengages, make sure you call his attention to you so you can click and treat him profusely. The more difficult this is for your dog, the better the rewards should be. You may have to walk a hundred feet away from this dog. So be it: the distance will decrease over time. If you find this to be too difficult, increase the value of your treat or toy, walk at a less busy time, and/ or do more of your car work before continuing with this part of the training. You must convince yourself that you can manage this task before taking it on.

There was a point during my rehabilitation with Acacia wherein she began to see other dogs from a distance and immediately run back and look up at me. Her tail would wag in a nervous way, and I would smile happily at her and praise her lavishly while moving away from the other dog if possible and/or necessary. She had learned by that time, to trust me!! It was truly a tearful moment for me because I realized that all my hard work was starting, after five weeks, to pay off! I still needed to provide her with a large safety distance from other dogs in order for her to feel safe, but over time that distance diminished.

Of course, we did have one major setback (and one giant heartbreak) when we were walking and a large, happy, black adolescent lab came bounding up to us off-leash. "He's friendly!" bellowed the owner from a football field away. There was nowhere to go. The lab simply wanted to play, but I could see the terror in Acacia's eyes. She looked up at me, wagged that nervous wag, and I tried to smile at her but I knew this was not going to go well. I was unable to be benevolent leader for her. I couldn't protect her. I had her on her leash, and I praised and treated her as best I could, but when that lab arrived and jumped right on her back, she growled, snapped, turned away, and looked at me with a face that begged me not to be angry with her. I praised her even more lavishly as we ran away from the yelping, now-receding lab. I felt awful that I couldn't help her allay her terror. But I think we both knew that we did the best we could. It was a stepping-stone toward better days. We really were a team, after all.

Some dogs are never going to be able to handle being near other dogs and be calm. Others will benefit greatly from associating loosely with very calm dogs. Our job at this point was to just learn to tolerate other dogs outside of a threshold distance. Over time, that distance became smaller. Once Acacia learned to see a dog and look at me, those dogs could be closer and closer. This didn't happen quickly; it took months. Eventually, if a dog was within about 20 feet, she'd express the desire to go sniff it. She wanted to interact with dogs but she often found them too excitable. Occasionally, however, we'd find a calmer dog, and I would be able to allow her to go sniff the behind of the other dog for a few seconds, then call her away. If her recall was good, I'd praise like crazy and move on. If her recall wasn't too good, I'd move away very happily and pretending to be lighthearted, but without yanking on her, and she'd disengage her attention from the other dog and come with me.

Acacia's body language helped me to gauge what she could tolerate in terms of stimuli. Even still, each time she sees another dog, her tail goes up like a flag. She whines and "honks" and stares at the other dog. Many of these behaviors used to indicate that she was over-stimulated by the dog, but now, some of these behaviors along with the "honking" noise, indicates that she wants to go visit. These days, her confrontational body language involves a hard stare and a growl, with a slowly moving flag tail. If I see these behaviors, visiting is not an option. If, while she is visiting, I see a hard stare and a still body, I know I need to call her away immediately. But if I see a still body with her face directed at the other dog but with her eyes averted, I know her next step is going to be a twisted pounce into a play bow.

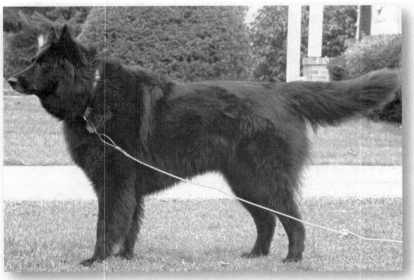

Acacia with ears up, staring and tail flagging. Not a friendly signal.

It took me a long time to learn these signals, but I realized that it took her an equally long time to figure them out, too! She needed time to learn which dogs were scarier and which were more likely to be calm. She needed time to learn that I was going to protect her and make decisions for her. Once she learned that, she began to relax in social situations. Butt sniffing is a very important canine behavior. When dogs greet, they sniff flews (sides of the mouth), ears, and butts. For Acacia, flews and ears were too scary because they are too close to eyes and teeth, but butts were acceptable. So as her threshold for distance grew smaller, I was able to select certain calm dogs who didn't seem to care too much whether their butts were being sniffed, and allow her to engage in this activity. Initially, when we approached one of these tolerant dogs, I'd give Acacia a cue to "go sniff." Once she was sniffing, I'd count to three. On three, I'd call her away and reward her. I might then send her back for a second sniff, then call her back again for a reward. Over time, she'd sniff for several seconds and then walk away; she desired no further interaction. That seemed to be all she wanted. That was fine with me!

For a while, I'd test her ability to tolerate more. I'd let her sniff the butt of a calmer dog, and if she wanted to sniff the ears, I'd let her. But it proved to be too much for her initially: if the other dog moved its head even slightly, Acacia would dive into her maniacal act. We needed to stop at butt sniffing for a while longer. She needed to feel safe near a dog before moving on to the next step. Faces are very scary for Acacia. If she goes for another dog, she goes for the face, and usually near the eyes. This is still an issue for her.

CALMING CURVES

If you are lucky enough to have access to a calm dog who doesn't really care about other dogs and who listens well to his owner, you can do an activity to work on your dog's reactivity to other dogs. I call

These dogs are learning that when they approach another dog, they turn away from it. The owners click when the dog commits to turning his head away, thereby teaching them calming signals.

it the calming curve. You need to start with your dogs on leash and at a distance from each other that will not elicit a response from your dog. At the same time, you will each take a step toward each other (I usually begin with three steps for each person), and then turn away from each other. At the apex of your turn, you will call your dog's name. When he turns his head away from the other dog, click and treat your dog. Your click is signifying that the turning of your dog's head away from the other dog is worthy of reward. You are teaching a calming signal. You are teaching your dog how to tell the other dog, and himself, that it doesn't really matter that the other dog is there.

Debby is loose-leash walking Elvis in a predetermined number of steps. When she reaches that number, she calls his name and then turns away. She clicks and treats as he turns his head away from the approaching dog. Note Elvis's focus on Debby's face as he turns away.

Repeat this activity several times, going back to the same starting point each time. Then increase the number of steps you each take toward each other before turning away (one at a time). During each training session, you will get a feel for how close your dog can get to the other dog before he begins to feel uncomfortable. He will indicate this (of course) through body language. If he strains at the leash, barks, stares, becomes stiff, or lunges, you know you've gotten too close too quickly. You will know that you are at the right distance when your dog is vigilant about the other dog but isn't losing it. He may give a long look, get a bit stiff, prick his ears, but still be able to turn away within a second or two. If his mouth is hard when taking treats, you're too close. Go back a few steps and get more successes at a farther distance, then stop the session.

This may be what happens if you get too close to quickly!

You will need to do this over several days, with different dogs, and in different environments before your dog really puts it all together. Using a confrontational dog as your assisting dog adds a huge challenge and is not advisable until much later on in your work.

Doing this work with a dog who has been socialized with other dogs as a puppy may require less time than if the dog hasn't played with other dogs early on. But this is a generalization. I knew that Acacia had played very nicely with other dogs as a pup and as an adolescent. I knew that she knew how to play appropriately. The prognosis for an under-socialized dog to play appropriately with other dogs is much poorer and is likely to take a much longer time.

As Bailey approaches a dog, his gate is stiff and erect, with tail up.
Linda calls him, and he is able to regain self-control, focus on her, and
walk away.

HUMANS: STRANGE BEASTS

What if your dog is reactive toward humans (or some subset thereof)? All of this talk about learning to deal with other dogs is fine, but if your dog freaks out over people, how does this strategy apply? The answer is, it's just the same.

Much of the work just described will apply to tolerance of and interaction with humans. There are a few exceptions.

At first, your dog will be crated if visitors come to the house. Make certain that your dog is safely contained and away from visitors, unless the visitors are humans that the dog knows well. When he rides in the car, he'll be crated and covered. People are everywhere. We need your dog to be calm and quiet for at least a week before teaching him some new responses.

You'll notice that sometimes your dog will react intensely to the sight of a person, and sometimes he may simply ignore the person. Why is this? Well, it could be for a number of reasons.

It would seem that dogs recognize and respond to the silhouette of an object in the process of recognition. A dog's cognizance of "human" includes an upright being with one head, an appendage on each side, and two legs on which he walks. They do usually see details on a person, but the quick recognition factor of a silhouette is important as a survival skill. Knowing this, it should be of no surprise that a human who is wearing a hat might be a cause of concern. The same may apply to glasses, beards, large coats, or boots, or a human carrying something. Umbrellas are objects that I routinely ask my students with small puppies to expose their pups to before age 16 weeks. A very large, overweight, or tall person may be disconcerting to a dog. It is just out of the "norm" for that particular dog.

Some of this issue goes back to socialization, but not all. When I brought Acacia home at age nine weeks, it was summer. Everyone she had ever seen in her little life wore shorts. I had her for a total of about three weeks when one evening I had a seminar to attend. She was upstairs with me while I dressed, and when she saw me wearing dark blue pants; she nearly threw herself down the stairs in fear. I somehow managed to scoop her up and hold her until she ceased shaking. It took nearly ten minutes. In this case, the overall appearance of "human" had changed, and it was terrifying. This is an example of a socialization-based issue.

This could also have been a fear period issue. Puppies undergo a number of fear periods wherein they become hypervigilant about their surroundings. These periods occur at variable times for each puppy,

The next step in working with reactivity to humans is to have the dog accept treats from the hand of the live bait, who is walking by. Note Match's eyes, front paw lift, and tail; all of which express concern.

and for varying periods of time. They serve as a tremendous survival tactic for canids in the wild because they coincide with increasing levels of independence in the pups. In effect, they teach the pups to be more and more leery of things they hadn't been exposed to so far. This increases the chance the pup will stay alive…but it can wreak havoc for domesticated dogs and their humans!

In some instances, a dog's fear of people may be based on pheromones. Hormonal mixes change in people during pregnancy, menstruation, during times of high stress or illness, or if they themselves are fearful. If a person is afraid of a dog, the dog is very likely to know it, and respond negatively to that person (i.e., if you're afraid of me, I'd better be leery of you!). The dog seems to perceive a fearful person as a "live cannon" and react in a confrontational manner.

Not only does the person's body language display tense, halting and/ or hesitating signals, but also the person's pheromones are screaming to the dog that all is not calm. If all is not calm, and the person's body language is odd (or other than calm), then the person must surely be the source of the problem. The dog's instinct is to defend itself against threats, and so the dog's behavior becomes threatening.

I can hear you asking, as you read this, why does MY dog do this, and no one else's dog do it? This is a common emotional response for owners of reactive dogs. There is no hard and fast answer to this question. Once in a while we are able to tease out a theoretical reason for reactivity. Perhaps the dog was a stray and had poor access to many stimuli. Perhaps the dog had been ill and became freaked out over people because of all of the medical treatment and the negative associations with pain and people. Often, however, it is a case of a potpourri of genetics, nutrition, socialization, personality, lifestyle, and exercise. Truly this is a vague answer to a burning question.

Match has learned that a person who walks by might have a treat for him, and he is calm enough to be able to focus on his owner and the passerby. Once the dog is this calm, he will be able to sit for treats from the live bait.

The reality is this: deal with the behaviors. Do not waste your time "psychologizing" your dog's reactivity. Avoid beating yourself up because you missed something in your dog's socialization period. Spend positive energy teaching positive new skills. Manage your dog while you are teaching new behaviors. You will be much more successful with your dog if you take this approach.

Let's return to that training session in the park where you got lovely attention from your dog upon emerging from the car. You begin your walk in the park, on a lesser-used trail. If you see a person from a distance, your training tactic will be identical to the one you just read about seeing another dog. All of those same rules apply, up to the butt sniffing! What's important here is that you make the decisions for your dog as to how close you will get to the person. Over time, your dog will learn that he doesn't need to worry about these decisions because you make them for him. He will heave a giant sigh of relief, thank you for taking care of it all, and go along his merry way.

Human beings have a difficult time recognizing a warning if they truly want something. There is going to be a person who, someday, will approach your dog and try to pet him. He may even ask you if he can pet your dog while rapidly approaching your now growling dog, without waiting for your permission or recognizing that your dog is threatening to bite him (or is hiding behind you). Often, this is a person who claims that he is "good with dogs; I've had dogs all my life." Help! What do you do?

I have learned the hard way that whether this is an adult, a child, or a person with a "friendly" dog, I need to be completely in control of the situation. There are times when I will come across as gruff, rude, bossy or mean. This is one circumstance wherein I don't mind being considered as such; it is MY responsibility to take care of my dog. I must keep my dog's best interests in mind. It is imperative for the safety of the other person, for the sanity of my dog, and for the health of my relationship with my dog (and for my wallet, in case I get sued). My dog is learning to trust in me; he's learning that I will take care of that scary stuff out there. Allowing a scary or threatening stimulus to cause my dog to cross her threshold of fear, if even for a second, puts my benevolent leadership at risk and undermines everything I've done up to this point.

Should a person approach you and ask to pet your dog, calmly inform them that your dog is afraid and is in training, and that perhaps if you see them in the future, they can help you train your dog, when he's ready. Then walk away. Do not continue to converse with the person or otherwise delay in this tactic, because the person is likely to do one of two things: sneer at you because you have a mean dog, or attempt to tell you the life history of every dog they've ever owned. Aside from being bored to tears over their pet escapades, you run the risk of taking your attention off of your dog. Your dog is not feeling safe; take him away to somewhere more calm and secure.

There may also be times when you'll just want to do an emergency U-turn. When you see a situation which concerns you, whether it be another dog approaching, multiple children, or noisy people, you may just want to treat them as if they are the other dog in a calming curve—call your dog and do a 180-degree pivot, going quickly and happily in the other direction. This may not always be an option if there's also activity behind you, but it sure can be a relief when you can do it. Always remember to party with your dog when he comes along with you.

When I started doing this, I felt embarrassed over having a dog who growled at people and dogs. People looked at me as if I mistreated my dog. They probably perceived me as being antisocial. No doubt it increased the challenge of the situation because my pheromones were a mess. Indeed, I spent nearly two years experiencing heartburn twice a day, during walk time. It was awful.

Needless to say, the day Acacia looked at a dog and then looked immediately back at me was the day I cried with happiness. There was hope! This is not an emotion you understand easily unless you've been there.

Live Bait

I've started this section on reactivity toward humans by suggesting that your dog be crated when visitors come to the house. I then summarized your work during your dog's outings in a park or other spacious area. This should be the sum of your dog's access to humans until your dog is able to walk with you within, say, 10-20 feet of a human. I am using these numbers as an average for the reactive dogs with whom I've worked. There will certainly be dogs for whom this distance is entirely too close, at least for a long time. I've also selected this distance because it is at this distance where those humans are going to be able to help in the process of counterconditioning and desensitizing the dog to humans.

At this point in your dog's career, you will need to have a human subject to assist you. I like to take as lighthearted an approach as possible in this sometimes emotional and demoralizing work, so I call this person "live bait." Let's set up a training session for your dog, using your live bait. Arm your live bait with lots of yummy, smelly treats that are larger in size than the treats you'd normally use for training. Try also to use a treat that will be visible (keeping in mind that your dog's spectrum of color perception includes black, white, purply-blues and orangy-yellows) against the color of the ground on which you will be working.

Agree to meet somewhere like a park or other wide-open space. You will bring your dog out of the car using the focus skills you learned earlier. Instruct your live bait to wait until you have rewarded your dog a number of times before appearing. As your live bait appears, you will continue to keep your dog's focus on you while your live bait walks past your dog. His distance from your dog should be as far as possible, while still being able to toss treats at your dog. He should aim for the front paws of your dog, and he should not look at your dog while doing this. His walking style should also appear to be relaxed, not hesitant or stiff. This requires some practice, as your live bait is now blindly tossing treats at a target! He will walk past your dog, not looking at your dog, and tossing treats at him **regardless of your dog's behavior;** you are using counterconditioning in this activity. Have your live bait repeat this action for several passes, back and forth.

Up until now, you've been working on having your dog focus on you, and for the most part, other people are ignoring, or keeping a wide berth from, your dog. But now, suddenly, this human is paying attention to him. There may not be eye contact or attempts to reach out and touch your dog, but he knows that this person is acknowledging his existence. This can be a significant and scary change of events for your dog, and he is likely to become reactive all over again, whether he is growling, barking or lunging at the person, or shaking and hiding behind you.

For a dog who finds people scary, using the classical conditioning method of "people=treats" helps a lot. Have a person walk by the dog at a distance which is minimally threatening to the dog and toss treats at the dog's front paws. Soon, the dog looks forward to an approaching person!

While your live bait is walking past you and tossing treats at your dog, you are continuing to ask your dog for behaviors which you can reward. Make certain that you maintain a sense of calm, happiness and confidence during these interactions. A more successful session would involve a dog who is so busy finding the treats on the ground that he barely looks up to look at the person. If this is the case, you will have little need to ask for a finger target or other skill. But don't think for a moment that your dog doesn't know that person is there! As a matter of fact, if you watch your dog's eyes, you'll likely see him watching the person as he's eating the treats. This is a good thing because the dog is associating calm (head down and food) with a scary stimulus. However, your session may be a bit less successful if your dog looks up at your live bait and reacts intensely. Should this occur, have your live bait toss several more treats in one or two more passes, and walk away. Take your dog back to the car and give him a break for a while until he is calm. You may either try this again or attempt it another day. You may also have your live bait toss treats from a farther distance, if possible.

The reason for tossing treats regardless of your dog's behavior is that we are counterconditioning your dog's response to a moving person who is showing some attention to him. This is a classical conditioning process, and as such, it is purely associative. Your dog's behavior is irrelevant. It is all about person=food, not about rewarding reactivity. This is a very difficult concept for many of my students to grasp. Fortunately, they usually do what I ask of them, and we soon find, after several sessions of this activity, that the dog becomes quiet and observant of the live bait. The dog learns that from "scary people" come "good things."

You will need to repeat each level for your dog several times. Once your live bait can walk by at 20 feet away, without looking at your dog, and toss treats, then turn around and walk back and toss treats again, and do this four or five times in a session, you've reached your first criterion. You really should take this slowly and do this in a few more sessions on different days before moving to a different level. You should also try to do this in different locales, or different areas of the park, to help the dog to generalize this concept a bit. Then have your live bait decrease his distance by two or three feet, and repeat it all.

There are so many variables to change over time in this process that it will be easy to miss some. However, keep in the front of your mind that distance and speed or intensity are the two main variables you will be changing in order to work with, and help your dog. Simply having your live bait wear a long sleeved shirt instead of a T-shirt, for example, can elicit a reactive response. If that happens, have your live bait work at a farther distance until your dog is calmer. In such cases, your dog's threshold is smaller (i.e., distance must be larger before he becomes reactive). Dogs are no different from people when it comes to having bad days and good days. Have patience. But always make certain that your live bait is safe from your dog, as well as that your dog feels safe from your live bait. Have a firm grip on your leash without choking your dog. Too much tension on your leash will impart the wrong message to your dog.

The next step in this walk-by activity is to have your live bait looking at your dog as he walks by and treats. When your dog is calm, your live bait can begin to talk happily but calmly to your dog as he walks by. Remember to go through each of the steps regarding distance before moving on to the next level. It will be easy to try to move too fast, and you will suffer setbacks as a result. You'll pay for it, too, because you'll need to go back and redo some of your work! Some trainers call this the "greedy trainer syndrome." We all do it!!! We try to accomplish too much too fast, and we end up making errors. Usually, it's not a big deal, but it does compromise your dog's trust a bit, and it ends up taking you more time.

At some point your live bait will be close enough to walk past your dog and start to deliver a treat right out of his hand. He should do this without stopping and, at least initially, without looking at or talking to your dog. When he does this, make certain that your live bait walks a straight line with his shoulder facing your dog. Body posture that indicates motion directly toward your dog is likely to result in a reactive response.

The next step in this process might include having your live bait stop briefly in front of your dog and ask him to sit. If he does, he should be treated and the live bait should quietly praise and walk away. This is important in the early stages because the scary human walking away is a reward for the dog. Pretty soon, though, the dog will look forward to the person approaching so he can sit for treats! Over time, your live bait may walk up to your dog (still from an angle), stop and ask your dog to sit, and then ask for several different behaviors which he can reward. The next step would be to increase the angle from which your live bait approaches, so that he eventually walks directly toward your dog. Because this can be so threatening, this step may take much work.

I cannot reiterate enough times how important it is to consider all of the variables that come into play in this process. Time of day, angle of approach, gender of live bait, type of clothing, whether there is another person or a dog nearby, mood, familiarity of the live bait, the list goes on. Just when you think you're making terrific progress, your dog will likely humble you by reacting. When this happens, just put him away in his car or crate and take a break. Likely, his reaction to the live bait was compounded by something else in his environment. Often, it will be something you can't identify. It's OK. You may want to stop your session for the day and come back to it another time.

HOME VISITS

Now back to your dog who's been crated when people come to visit. This is not a preferred final scenario for two reasons. First, we want our dog to be a part of the family. Second, crating your dog is not teaching him appropriate behavior while greeting guests; it's management. Now that we've had a chance to work on people and dogs as overwhelming stimuli, we can start to teach new behaviors at home. The work you've done out in public is somewhat easier because you can create the appropriate distance from stimuli to accommodate your dog's threshold. In the house, that distance is much smaller, and therefore, more difficult to work with.

The work you will do in the house is similar to what you've just done in the park or out for a walk. Start with a live bait person who elicits only a mild reaction from your dog. Have your dog in his crate, which is in another room, when the person arrives so you can discuss what you're going to practice. Then bring your dog out of his crate when he's calm and quiet and get his focus onto you. If he's barking, whining, scratching or howling, ignore him and enjoy your visit until he's quiet. Start by working your dog as far away as possible from the live bait. Do as many skills as you can with your dog, knowing that he will turn to check out the stranger. This is fine, so long as he's not reacting. Understand that you only want to allow him to gaze, if that tends to be his response, at the person for a maximum of three seconds before you call him away. We want him to look at the live bait and decide it's important for him to check in with you. At first, stop after only a few rewarded behaviors, and then have a party and put him away. Enjoy your success!

The next step in this challenge is to be able to sit down and have your dog pay attention to you while you talk to the guest. Your dog will be best to lie down for these sessions because laying down calms the dog down and calms down others in the room. This is definitely an activity you should practice regularly, at home, on leash, without guests, until your dog enjoys the activity, prior to adding the guest. You can do targets, stays, and other tricks like "head down" or "paw." Keep these sessions short at first, and then increase them. Look for signs of stress in your dog and end before he starts to become antsy or agitated. Stopping a session when your dog is agitated reinforces agitation because it makes the "scary" thing stop, thereby reducing the anxiety. It also doesn't teach anything new.

Acacia lies down on her bed and receives treats from me and our visitor. No way is she getting off that bed; the treats would stop! The leash is short enough that the dog can't reach the visitor, thereby providing security for both.

While you are doing these sessions, have your live bait tossing treats at your dog. Chances are, your live bait's toss is going to miss your dog at some point and your dog will have to get up to get the treats. That's fine; just ask him for a down again and reward that. Pretty soon, your dog will be looking at your guest quietly, waiting for treats. Over the next sessions your live bait will be able to sit closer. Be careful about how quickly you diminish the safe distance. Don't be a greedy trainer! Having the humans sitting down puts them at risk, should the dog feel too threatened. Go slow on this one. In these sessions, the visitor is already in the room when the dog appears, and remains in the room until after the dog leaves.

Initially, you will probably need to either call your dog as the live bait stands up to redirect his attention to you so you can reward him, or have both you and your live bait pelt him with treats as your live bait stands up. When you achieve an 80% success rate at this level, your live bait can soon begin to walk around and toss treats, much like he did in the park. When your guest stands up, make sure he's at a farther distance than he was while he was sitting, at least initially. Eventually he'll be able to approach the dog and ask for a sit, perhaps pet him on the cheek, and give a treat. Remember, a moving person is more stimulating than a sitting or nonmoving person, so you may see some regression when you do this part. You'll want to spend a long time doing this before trying to do this at the door when the guest arrives.

Should your dog at any point react by barking or growling, calmly take him back to his crate. You do not want your dog to rehearse that behavior. Either wait until he is calm and quiet, and then try again with the person at a farther distance, or end the session for the day. Remember, when you do take your dog back to his crate, do so with a calm and gentle demeanor, and always give a little treat for going into the crate. There is, however, no discussion during the transition.

When you are implementing these training strategies, you will be most efficient and most confident if you use a chart or graph of some sort so that you can keep track of what you've been doing and what your dog has been doing. Whether you are working on reactivity toward another dog, toward people outside, or toward a person coming into your home, it's a long, multi-step process. Even if you **think** your dog is doing well, don't push it! Dealing with reactivity is a process; we are changing the underlying emotional response to stimuli. It simply cannot change overnight, or even in a week or a month. The stimuli that your dog reacts to may change. The seasons change, and with it, peoples' clothing. The scents on the ground and in the air change, as do human and other animal pheromones. Any or some or all of these variables may make a difference, and sometimes it's difficult to impossible to predict and work away from them.

BRAIN MELT

While we're at it, we need to go over the nature of learning curves. This is a predictable and often frustrating phenomenon that you need to understand as you work on rehabilitating your dog. When you begin to teach your dog a skill, it appears as if he understands it. It seems like the proverbial light bulb is going on. Then, all of a sudden, he acts as if he has no clue what you want him to do. He may offer other behaviors to explore whether they will result in the same rewards. This is called, "sampling." Alternatively, he may ignore you, walk away, sniff the ground, or look away. This, to me, is a sign that what you are asking may be too difficult for him at that particular time. He may also simply shut down and do nothing. When any of these happens, calmly go back to the step before and reward for any appropriate response. Get some good responses to this level of ability before going back to the level at which he had difficulty. Once he's back to the new level, he will have it for a while, and then he'll likely have another bout of uncertainty, but it should last a shorter period of time and require less help. We refer to these little spasms in your dog's learning curve as "dips" in the learning curve. There are usually two of them per skill; the first is larger than the second. Once you understand this phenomenon, teaching new skills becomes somewhat easier and less frustrating, and it's fun to see it taking place and predicting what's going to happen next!

Over time, you will begin to work your dog for longer periods of time and in more distracting and challenging situations. You may begin to take your dog to the pet food store, or to the park when there are many other dogs or children playing soccer. You may think your dog is doing great, and then suddenly, Whamo! Your dog freaks out over a stimulus that hasn't bothered him since the very beginning of time. It's devastating. It's upsetting. You will feel like you have spent all this time and effort for nothing.

Relax. Take a breath. This is normal. While it would be a waste of time to try to "psychologize" what happened, you may take this approach: somewhere along the way, your dog's reactive stimuli accumulated to the point where they exceeded his threshold. It's that simple.

How do we help to prevent this from happening? It's fairly simple. If you feel that you've had a wonderful day with your dog, you've taken him somewhere and you wondered whom this dog was and what did they do with **your** dog, because he was so well behaved, give him a break. Leave him at home for the next day or maybe even two. Restrict his outdoor exercise to something remote and quiet, as you did in the beginning. Let some of those glucocorticoids diminish in his system. He may appear to be calm and relaxed, but look carefully at his body during his successful interactions. You may see that his eyes are still large, or his mouth is still a little hard when taking treats. His lips may quiver or be pulled back a bit. There may be a bit of drool or excess panting going on. To the casual observer, your dog may appear to be calm, cool, and collected when in fact, he's doing a great job of covering it up. He's been learning some wonderful tools in order to accomplish that, but that doesn't mean there isn't still some anxiety attached. His work of counterconditioning his emotional responses is not yet finished.

So give him a day off. In addition, take him for long, quiet walks or runs to more quickly eliminate all those stress hormones. There will be another day in which to accomplish more.

IN A CLASS BY ITSELF

There are so many reactive dogs in this world. Why is that? I believe it is because we have so many more people, so much more breeding of dogs and therefore more stretching of genetic material, more crowding and stimuli in general, more pollution and poorer ingredients in dog foods. Dog laws in most communities do not encourage concepts such as early socialization and the acceptance of dogs in the general population.

Do you disagree with this statement? Think about it. In the USA, dogs are usually not allowed in restaurants, schools, grocery stores and shops in general. Many parks don't allow dogs. No dogs are permitted in any of our fine National Parks except for the parking areas. Leash laws exist in nearly every community, and most of us with dogs either have or want fencing in order to easily contain our dogs when they need to go out and relieve themselves. Many of us wouldn't be caught walking our dogs. And then there's the electric fencing. Many owners who install this equipment place it in their front yards, right down to the sidewalk! Their dogs have lots of opportunity to see things, but can't get to any of them. What a tease! Worse yet, people and dogs on the outside of the fence can tease them. They can see it but can't get to it. How, then, do they get the socialization necessary for proper adjustment to their world? Veterinarians often tell their clients to avoid taking their puppy anywhere until they have completed their entire set of vaccinations. That's at age 16 weeks...the end of the prime socialization period!

Some of the worst cases of canine reactivity that I've seen have been dogs who live in apartment complexes. These dogs are subjected to a constant barrage of stimuli. All day long, they hear people coming and going, walking around upstairs, slamming doors, people talking or shouting. They hear and smell other dogs, and cats as well. They usually have the opportunity to look out the windows that overlook the parking lot or a main entrance. Again, they have the chance to see the stimuli but have little or no chance to interact with it. These are the dogs with whom I must work the longest, and with the least change over time. For them, the mere prospect of existing is overwhelming. Obviously, these dogs started out with compromised genetic material, and other issues have compounded it.

So what can be done for all of these dogs?

I run classes for dogs just like the ones I've been describing all this time. It's called Reactive Class. There are a few of them around the country and we all run our classes somewhat differently. I'd like to take a bit of time to outline how I run my classes in the hopes that other trainers may be able to take the framework and begin to offer them in their area.

I have a maximum of five dogs per class, and each class runs approximately 1 hour and 30 minutes. I prefer to run these classes outside and in a large area. My training studio has a large and rather remote parking lot attached to it, and we use this area for our classes in decent weather. Once we get snow and single digit temperatures, however, we move the classes inside until the weather breaks again. There are pro's and con's to both locations.

Each dog/person team that comes to class has completed a minimum of three private lessons. During these lessons, a complete history of the dog and his reactive triggers is taken, and the owner learns how to manage the dog while teaching new skills such as finger or hand targeting, sits, downs, leave-its, and other tricks. They also begin to understand the choreography of the Reactive Class, as it is such a strange class! Before they can begin to attend the class, the humans must come to the class at least one time without their dogs so that they can see what it's like, and so that there are no surprises when they begin. They have the opportunity to meet classmates and learn that theirs is not the only reactive dog in the world. If we're working inside, the dog also has the emotional advantage of having been in the room, and worked in the room, before. We then can use that person as live bait!

When the class is being run outside, we all meet in the parking lot, with our cars parked as far away from each other as possible. I strongly encourage students to crate and cover their dogs. If they refuse or if the car doesn't lend itself toward crating, we cover the windows with towels and blankets. We all get out of our cars and have a pow-wow. We each give brief weekly reports of our dogs, including successes and failures, and any new tricks taught or major life changes. This is truly a support group for folks who love their dogs and are very dedicated to them. There are times we hate our dogs' behavior and complain about it, and there are also times we are so proud of them that we can't wait to boast! We then orchestrate what we are going to do with each dog during that lesson. I have a Yahoo group for members of this class, and much of this discussion takes place on the list so as to avoid leaving our dogs in hot or cold cars, and to maximize the amount of actual work that gets done.

We then proceed in getting one dog out of the car at a time. We work with that dog according to his triggers. Sometimes the dog can't get out of the car without barking or ignoring his owner. I've had at least one dog who wasn't able to get out of the car for several months' worth of weekly classes because she was too fearful and barky. Sometimes the dog needs to be very far away from people and/or dogs, and sometimes we do "send-offs." A send-off is when the dog is sitting next to or near the owner and paying attention to him. Another person approaches, and the owner tells the dog, using a directional finger point, to "go see" or "go visit." The dog goes toward the visiting person, who has picked up the vector of the owner's finger target and continues it, bringing it in toward himself. As soon as he does this, he asks the dog to sit. Once the dog sits, he can be clicked and treated. Sometimes the dog may stay there and receive extra treats for continuing a sit, or the visitor may ask the dog to do some of his tricks.

Jen "sends-off" Sammy to target my finger.

Once the visitor is finished with the visit, he sends the dog back to his owner in the same manner as he received him, with a finger target and a "go see." Should the dog bark or not sit, the visitor either ignores the dog while the owner calls the dog back, or the visitor may walk away if the dog tries to jump on the visitor.

Each dog/person team usually gets two turns to work per lesson. The sessions may last anywhere from ten seconds to ten minutes. While this may not seem like much stage time, it can be overwhelming for the dog, and I'm sure for the owner, particularly those who are new to the class. The dogs often are exhausted after class, and sometimes they shut down after the first session and indicate that they don't want to work for the second one. We respect that, and understand that some critical learning has just taken place.

We combine exercises which include having the dog be still while people and/or other dogs move around at "beyond threshold" distances, as well as having the dog move around while other people and/or dogs stay still. We try to make as much use of tricks and motion as possible. It is best to avoid having the dog stay still for long periods of time, as it builds anxiety and is more likely to result in a reactive response.

Emmet is learning that people are predictors of treats, so he wants to interact with them. But Marcie calls him away because if he makes eye contact for more than a few seconds, he'll make the wrong decision..

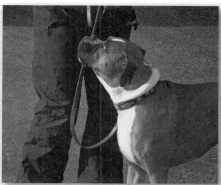

Jaxson is distracted by another dog. Barb calls his name and he re-focuses on her. Note the loose leash.

Some dogs work on desensitizing more than one trigger per session, while others work on one for several weeks and then a different one for several weeks, the move back to the first one. This is where reactive dog work becomes an art. Being able to read body language, understanding what is likely to be perceived as boring, and perceiving stimuli are critical to being successful in running these classes. I am not always perfect and I make mistakes. It can be exhausting work for me, for my students, and for my dogs.

If the classes are run inside, we all meet and go inside and leave our dogs in their cars. We discuss the past week's events, make a plan for our lesson, and proceed. Usually there is one dog in the room at a time. The goal is always to have all of the dogs in the building at the same time. My training studio has a long, quiet hallway that is little used, a lobby, an office, and the main room. I use all of it! We bring in one dog, get some successful behaviors, and have him leave and bring in the next one. Again, we go as far as we can with the dog without having him exceed the threshold of reactivity. Often, the dogs respond best to coming in briefly, checking it out, then leaving and coming back in again a few minutes later. It seems to diminish the "arrival anxiety," which so many of them (and us) seem to experience.

We make use of the exercises I outlined in this book, including calming curves, tossing food as we walk by, doing send-offs, and asking for tricks. If a dog has reached a level of calm that allows him to pay very good attention to his owner, we may engage him in some free-shaping while other things are happening in the room. This

Abby needs to enter the training studio, exit, and re-enter it several times in order to be able to handle a beautiful entrance like this one.

Gerda finds certain stimuli scary, such as backpacks, umbrellas, and bicycles. Silhouettes are scary if they are "different." Here, Sam is with a "scary'" bicycle and tossing Gerda a treat. Note that Gerda's weight is still on her back legs.

In this send-off, I am sending Abby back to Jeannette after having her sit in front of me for a treat and petting. Using my finger target as a directional hand signal, I point to Jeannette, who uses her finger target to get Abby back to sitting in front of her.

is a very cool process. I always get excited when a dog is able to do free-shaping in reactive dog class because it means that the dog has learned to focus on a cool learning activity and leave the extraneous stimuli alone. We also make use of the agility equipment in the room, working on one piece at a time. This keeps it interesting but not highly exciting, which is all-important to a reactive dog in a potentially scary situation.

Occasionally, we will take some time to work on a new trick or to talk more about free-shaping. Dogs who are new to the class are not good candidates for free-shaping unless they've done it before. This is because free-shaping is, in itself, anxiety producing in the beginning. The dog doesn't understand what's being asked of him; he must figure that out for himself. Once he's been successful a few times at the process, he will be more likely to be able to handle maintaining his focus on his owner and on the task at hand. A dog who isn't sure of the expectation is likely to look around, and in this environment, that is **not** a preferable activity.

DOGS ON DRUGS

In our world of pharmaceutical obsession, it's not surprising that we have drugs for our pets who suffer from anxiety. While everything has its place, it also has its limits. Many veterinarians have placed their patient dogs on psychotropic medications. The results have been variable. The reason is that, in many cases, the prescribed medication is a guess. There are several classes of medications: tri-cyclic antidepressants, anxiolytics, selective serotonin-reuptake inhibitors (SSRIs), barbiturates, etc. It is the prescribing veterinarian's responsibility to know which is the most appropriate. While a board-certified veterinary behaviorist is most likely to be able to make such a judgment, they are few and far between (fewer than 50 worldwide). Most dog owners are unaware that a veterinary behaviorist is their best choice or they are unwilling to unable to travel to one, so they rely on their local vet for help. Few veterinarians have an interest or the background in behavior medicine necessary to make an educated decision about medications, but some will prescribe a medication at the owner's request, and "see what happens."

Sometimes they strike it lucky; other times there is no benefit. Occasionally, damage is done by using the wrong medication.

It is important to understand that these medications do not remove fear, which is the basis for much anxiety. An anxiolytic (anti-anxiety) medication will alter the neurochemical mix in the brain, which will allow new things to be learned. This requires time and behavior modification.

In my career, I have found only a few clients whose dog's reactivity improved with the use of medication. That is not to say they aren't out there; it just hasn't been my experience. Having said that, it is important to recognize that sometimes a veterinary visit is helpful in pinpointing the cause of some illness or discomfort which may contribute to your dog's reactivity. If you would like to find a board-certified veterinary behaviorist, you can visit www.dacvb.org.

THE TAIL END

Having a reactive dog can be a mortifying, upsetting, embarrassing, and frustrating ordeal. It can really wear you down and make you question why you own a dog. I wrote this book because I endured all of those emotions as I watched Acacia's reactivity unfold, and I felt compelled to share my learning process with others who have experienced or are experiencing a similar situation.

You should be able to follow the suggestions and recommendations outlined here with relative ease. But your best chance of effectively rehabilitating your reactive dog is in finding a caring, knowledgeable positive trainer and a Reactive Dog Class. The first one may be easier to find than the second. Where you do find such services?

As a staunch supporter of the Association of Pet Dog Trainers (APDT), your first move should be to visit their website at *www. apdt.com*. Do their trainer search; you should be prepared to travel two hours or more to find a trainer who fits the bill. Make sure to interview the trainer of interest to be sure that he or she is familiar with working with reactive dogs, *and* that only positive reinforcement and negative punishment are being used. If the trainer talks about dominance or alpha, or if there is mention of choke chains, prong collars or shock collars, hang up or walk away! Membership in APDT does not guarantee that a trainer is positive.

Other designations you can look for are CPDT (Certified Professional Dog Trainer), membership in the IAABC (International Association of Animal Behavior Consultants), or a CDBC (Certified Dog Behavior Consultant). These designations indicate that a trainer has logged a certain number of training hours and has a sound working knowledge of behavior science. However, none of these guarantees that the trainer will use only positive, nonconfrontational training techniques.

The terms I use in this book are not peculiar to dog trainers; they are based in science. Call or email trainers and ask them what experience they have in working with reactive dogs. Ask if you may watch a group class; any class will do as a start. You need to feel comfortable with the person you're going to trust to help you. Talk to students as they're coming to or leaving class, and ask them how they like the classes and the instructor.

Dog training is not a regulated industry, so it is critical that you find someone you like and trust. If the trainer is not well versed in the language of behavior modification, or if he will not permit you to watch a class, walk away. Do not entertain any conversation that includes choke chains, prong collars, shock collar, spray bottles, or other punishment. It is bad news for a reactive dog. Also dismiss a trainer who offers to take your dog and board him and train him for you. You need to build a working relationship between *you* and *your dog*; no trainer can do that work for *you*.

The support of others who were going through the same concerns as me proved to be invaluable. Walking my dog every day, dealing with barking, lunging, growling, and the stares and comments of others who didn't understand took a toll on me. I started to hate my dog before I began my Reactive Dog Class. Now I not only love my dog, I'm very proud of her accomplishments. If you have a trainer you like and trust, but doesn't run a class for reactive dogs, ask her if she would be willing to start such a class.

A reactive dog will always be a reactive dog. There is no "fixing" such a dog. The activities and information outlined here will assist you in managing and training your dog. Some of them are skills that your dog will learn and which, over time, will be easier to do and will be more automatic responses for both you and your dog. Others are types of management that can never be eliminated. Acacia will always have to be on a leash when she goes out the front door; otherwise, she will likely target any moving thing, chase it and probably scare it. It is not worth testing whether she will bite it. It would be unreasonable to believe that because my dog has a wonderful skill set and trust in me as her benevolent leader that I can trust her to make appropriate decisions about the world around her.

That doesn't mean that I love her less. Because I've mentioned Acacia so many times, I'll update you on her progress. I no longer have to walk her on a leash or a long line in most of the places we go for hikes. We frequent about five or six different places regularly; most of them are large parks with hiking trails. There are areas where I will leash her as a precaution. We always practice recalls when we see people or bikes or dogs coming, and just as often we practice for the heck of it when no one is around. She always gets rewarded with treats. Lately, she has become ball-obsessed, which is nice because her attention is focused more on balls than anything else. It makes my job easier. When she comes across another dog, she still flags her tail, but her noises indicate excitement and a real desire to greet and play. Some of her best friends are Labs, particularly chocolate Labs. Occasionally she will get into a scuffle with another dog; usually the dog's greeting has been more direct or excitable than she can tolerate. She finds playtime in all classes but one too stimulating and asks me to take her out. The group with whom she plays is a group of dogs she's known and played with singly or in small groups for nearly a year. Her inner group of trusted humans has grown exponentially as well. She still distrusts strangers (as Belgians often do) but will growl, sniff and walk away as a rule. I've become convinced that her eyesight is poor, and I treat her accordingly. I believe there is little reason to test it because I'd treat her the same way anyway. Acacia is active in Rally-O, agility, and herding, and does occasional visits as a therapy dog at a nursing home. She has yet to display inappropriate behavior in that capacity. She thrives on being my demo dog in group classes.

Second Edition Update:
Acacia is now ten years old, and has become a most wonderful dog! She never titled in herding and I stopped doing Therapy Dog work with her because she didn't like it. She is my partner when I do presentations at schools, though, and loves being "on stage." She occasionally trials in agility, even at her old age, but she has really excelled in Rally-0! As this writing, her titles are: Can CH ARCHEX Acacia HIC, CGC, TDI, R1 MCL, R2 MCL, RL3X, RN, RL1X, RL2X2

She has taught my younger Belgian Sheepdog some bad habits but she has also taught him some great things, too. She is even more reliable off leash than ever, is often a real social butterfly with individual dogs, but is still overwhelmed in groups of dogs.

While Acacia did not turn out to be the wonder dog I had hoped she would become, I love her dearly and I'm very proud of the work we have done together. In short, she created her own version of "Wonder Dog," and that's good enough for me!

She has bravely learned to trust me without question. Without her, I wouldn't be half the trainer I am now. Once I began my odyssey with her, I realized that her role in my life was to humble the trainer.

Thank you, Acacia.

It is now your turn, perhaps, to open the pages to the world of your dog. It will be frustrating, for sure. But allow yourself to watch your dog learn new skills, and learn to trust you, and you will cry with happiness on the day your dog turns to you to ask for help. It will make you whole again, and give you new meaning to the word, "companion."

This is what it's all about! Acacia truly has learned to trust me. Finally.

ACKNOWLEDGEMENTS

I am the sort of person who really hates the acknowledgement section of books. I rarely read them. But I understand that the writer needs to thank certain people for the loving and tireless help of those around him. I suppose I suddenly find myself no different.

Acacia. The thorn tree. What an appropriate name. Acacia is a Belgian Sheepdog. She came to me at nine weeks, full of fire. We soon nicknamed her, "piranha dog." Little did I know what I was in for as she grew. Acacia moved my status from being a budding trainer who was determined to never use positive punishment with her, to a wise trainer who is able to help others with reactive and difficult dogs (and who still doesn't use positive punishment). The dog is the teacher; the teacher is the student.

Montana. Our Founder. Montana, a Border Collie mix, crossed the Rainbow Bridge three days shy of 16 years, and came to me as a 4-year-old shelter dog. She was "the magical dog." She was almost always perfect in her ways. She was a social equalizer for puppies, she never jumped, never stole things, never needed a leash. She was my experiment for every training technique known to man. She endured it all, and thanked me when I found clicker training. She loved the car, loved a good walk, and had crisscrossed the country with me more than once. She was a wise old soul. Everyone should be so lucky to have a girl like Montana.

The first human I need to thank is Carolyn Wilki. She is a friend and a mentor. She is a trainer and a very intelligent person. Without her knowledge and unfailing support, I would not still have Acacia. The first time Acacia bit a person, I made excuses for her. The second time she bit, I drove the 45 minutes up to Carolyn's sheep farm and cried on her shoulder for two hours while I decided whether to put the dog to sleep or work with her. I am so glad to have had the perfect person to help me make that decision. Sometimes I felt a bit guilty because I allow Carolyn to go off and do all sorts of reading, and then I learn from her and use the newly gleaned information! Hey, but what are friends (and mentors) for?

The second person I owe unending thanks to is my husband, and best friend, Pete Smoyer. Pete's the sort of person who is always there to help. He never questions, never complains. Without his giant hands to help, my business would not be what it is, and my book would not be written. Regardless of what it is that we do, we have a good time together. My dogs are insanely in love with him, and he them. It's a wonderful thing. Love you, Pedro.

From there, the list branches out.

My family, who always questioned and doubted me but underneath it all, knew I'd be just fine. We fight like a family, and hide much of the good energy. But we all love each other.

Carolyn Clark. You'd never guess you'd be on this list! You were "my competition," in my eyes. As a brand-new trainer in Ottawa, Ontario, I perceived you as "the one to beat"! When I brought Acacia to you for puppy class, I had my back up. You held your arms out. You were the pivot point in my transition from choke chains to clickers. How could I possibly forget?

My cyber-friend, Tess Stinson, who pressed me to write more! MORE!!, on the topic that helped her out with her Belgian Malinois Rocket and Greta, and the line of fosters she nurtures. Little did I know that she's a professional proofreader! Thank you, Tess.

Friends and students. They change over time, but they provide the love and support and encouragement to put pen to paper (or fingers to keyboard) and spread the message that I am compelled to share. Pauline, Deb, Sue, Pams (many of them!), Val and Jim, Jenna. Each one of you has pushed me to learn more, to read more, to teach more. Thank you, all.

REFERENCES AND RESOURCES

REFERENCES

1. Skinner, B.F., *About Behaviorism*, New York, Random House, 1974.

2. Sapolsky, Robert M., *Why Zebras Don't Get Ulcers*, New York, Henry Holt & Company, LLC, 1998.

3. Rugaas, Turid, *On Talking Terms with Dogs: Calming Signals*, Wenatchee, WA, Dogwise Publishing, 2006

4. Coppinger, Raymond and Lorna, *Dogs: A Startling New Understanding of Canine Origin, Behavior & Evolution*, New York, Scribner, 2001.

5. Tellington-Jones, Linda, *Unleash Your Dot's Potential DVD*, North Pomfret, VT, Trafalgar Square Publishing, 2005

6. Helen Graham and Gregory Vlamis, *Bach Flower Remedies for Animals*, Findhorn, Scotland, Findhorn Press, 1999.

7. I like to attribute the term, "stuff-a-dog" to Carolyn Wilki. Carolyn Wilki is a professional dog trainer in Bangor, Pa. She teaches pet obedience and herding as well as works with dog reactivity and aggression. She can be reached by phone at 610 LUV LAMB.

RESOURCES

The Association of Pet Dog Trainers (APDT) is the largest international association of dog trainers who are dedicated to using dog-friendly training. The APDT supports the ongoing education of trainers, other animal professionals and the public. Visit their website at www.apdt.com.

For more help with crate training:
Anderson, Teoti, *Quick and Easy Crate Training*, Neptune City, NJ, TFH Press, 2005.

For general training advice:
Miller, Pat, *The Power of Positive Dog Training*, Hoboken, Howell Book House, 2008.
Miller, Pat, *Positive Perspectives: Love Your Dog, Train Your Dog*, Wenatchee, WA, Dogwise Publishing, 2004.

For more help with reactivity:
McDevitt, Leslie, *Control Unleashed: Creating A Focused and Confident Dog*, South Hadley, MA, Clean Run Productions, 2007.

For information on relationship building with your dog:
Clothier, Suzanne, *Bones Would Rain from the Sky: Deepening Our Relationships with Dogs*, New York, Warner Books, 2005.
McConnell, Patricia, *The Other End of the Leash*, New York, Ballantine Books, 2002.
McConnell, Patricia, *For the Love of a Dog: Understanding Emotion in You and Your Best Friend*, New York, Ballantine Books, 2007.

INDEX

V